U.S. Outline Maps
&
State Studies

*Ready-to Use
Maps
Questions
&
Research Activities*

WRITTEN BY
RANDY L. WOMACK, M.ED.
ILLUSTRATED BY
CHRISTINA "CHRIS" LEW

PUBLISHED BY

G.E.C. PUBLICATIONS

"LEADING THE WAY IN CREATIVE EDUCATIONAL MATERIALS" ™

857 LAKE BLVD. ❖ REDDING, CALIFORNIA 96003

TO TEACHERS AND PARENTS

This book, *U.S. Outline Maps & State Studies*, was written as a complete resource for you to use by itself and/or along with your regular history, social studies and/or geography programs. This is an excellent book for introducing children to the different states, and encouraging them to continue learning more about each individual state and our great country.

This book contains 54 reproducible maps of the United States, Washington, D.C. and the fifty individual states. The maps of the United States show the *Political Boundaries, Major Waterways* and *Outline*. We have included a *generic* question sheet — STATE QUESTIONS — that can be used with all of the states. In addition to that, we have included an ADDITIONAL ACTIVITIES page, which will help guide some of the students in a more in-depth study and research of the states.

Each individual state has an activity/information page and outline map. The first page is a factual list of important statistics, information and historical events. The facing page is an outline map of the state. Have your students fill in relief symbols, cities, counties or anything else you feel is important.

Besides learning geography, children who use this book will grow in self-confidence and worth. Confusion, frustration and defeat often come to children when too much is drawn on a map — as you have probably realized if you have ever tried to read an atlas. We have deliberately simplified the maps because it is much easier for children to visually discriminate one item at a time, i.e., neither longitude nor latitude lines, etc. This will allow you, as the teacher, to determine what the student should study using a particular map. You can also make copies of the maps and introduce something different at a later time.

In making two-dimensional maps, there are always problems with scaling the maps down, North-South orientation and the complexity of the earth's coastline. Taking these things into consideration, and most importantly, the needs of the students, we deliberately scaled the maps to the page and not to the other states.

It is our hope that when you use the activities in this book, that you and your students will have fun as you become more familiar with each of the states of the United States. Thanks for using our book.

Randy & Chris
AUTHOR & ARTIST

Copyright ©1997 Golden Educational Center
©1992 All Rights Reserved – Printed in U.S.A.
©1990 Published By Golden Educational Center
857 Lake Blvd. ❖ Redding, CA 96003

Notice
Reproduction of worksheets by the classroom teacher for use in the classroom and not for commercial sale is permissible.

No part of this publication may be reproduced, stored in a retrieval system, or transmitted, in any form or by any means, electronic, mechanical, recording or otherwise, without written permission of the publisher.

Reproduction of these materials for an entire school, or for a system or district is strictly prohibited.

ISBN 1-56500-019-6

State Questions

Name _____ Date _____

State Name _____ Abbreviations: _____ _____
                                                Traditional   Postal Use

1. About how many people live in the state? _____

2. What is the area of land in square miles? _____

3. Name the highest mountain or elevation and how many feet it is above sea level.
   _____

4. In what region of the United States is this state located? _____

5. This state joined the Union on _____ as the _____ state.

6. Name the largest city and its population. _____

7. _____ became the capital city in _____.

8. This state is considered part of the _____ states.

9. What percentage of people live in the city? _____ Non-city? _____

10. What was the state's first non-Indian permanent settlement? _____
    _____

11. Explain why you think the historical event was important to the particular state and/or the entire United States. _____
    _____
    _____

12. Write one or two paragraphs about the industries, agriculture and/or the natural resources where you live and why they are important to you and your community. (Use more paper if you need to.)
    _____
    _____
    _____
    _____
    _____

© Golden Educational Center

U.S. Outline Maps & State Studies

Additional Activities

Name _____

Date _____

State Name _____

You may need to use an encyclopedia or other resource book to complete the following activities on separate sheets of paper.

1. Arrange the states in order of area, with the largest being number one.
2. Arrange the states in order of population, with the largest being number one.
3. Arrange the states in order of the density of population, with the denses being number one.
4. Arrange the states in the order they were admitted to the Union.
5. List all of the states where a president was born. Write the name or names of the presidents next to the state where they were born.
6. Write a paragraph or two describing the schools in the state.
7. Write a paragraph or two describing the state's climate and seasons.
8. Make a map of all of the major waterways in the state.
9. Make a map plotting all of the cities listed in the state's word search.
10. Write two or three paragraphs describing the state's natural resources. Explain why you think these resources are important.
11. Draw and color a picture of the state's flag. Write what the symbols and colors stand for on separate piece of paper.
12. Make a relief map of the state, showing all of the land regions. Write a short paragraph describing each of the regions.
13. In a report, tell about the state's agriculture and how it affects the economy.
14. Write one or two paragraphs about the industries of the state.
15. Make a map showing the symbols and locations of the farm and forest products.
16. If you can find a map showing the rainfall and/or the temperatures in winter and summer, copy them onto your own map(s).
17. Find pictures of the state animals and plants and draw your own pictures of them. Write a paragraph or two about each one you draw.
18. Research some of the most important historical events that took place and write a short report about them. Draw pictures to go along with your report.
19. Write a two or three page report about the history of the state. If possible, draw pictures and maps to go along with your report.
20. Interview someone who has lived in the state and find out their favorite places to go and things to do.
21. Make a list of the professional sports teams and their home states. Write the names of the cities where the teams play. Plot the cities and teams on a U.S. state boundary map.
22. Draw pictures of a sports team's mascot. Write a report about the mascot and/or the team's history.

© Golden Educational Center

U.S. Outline Maps & State Studies

United States

Name _____

Date _____

Independence: Declared on July 4, 1776. It was actually won on October 19, 1781, by defeating Great Britain in the Revolutionary War.

Capital City: Washington, D.C. (District of Columbia). The capital was named after Christopher Columbus and George Washington.

Area: 3,539,846 square miles.   Ranks 4th in the world in size and 3rd in population.

Population (1994 est.): 250,077,000 people.   **Density:** 70 people per square mile.
   Distribution: 74% urban (city).   26% rural (non-city).

National Motto: In God We Trust. Adopted July 30, 1956.

Some Highests ❖ Lowests ❖ Mosts of the United States.

Largest City: New York (New York state) — approximate population is 7,350,000 people.

Highest Elevation: Mt. McKinley, Alaska — 20,320 feet above sea level.

Lowest Elevation: Death Valley, California — 282 feet below sea level.

Deepest Gorge: Hells Canyon of the Snake River, Idaho — 7,900 feet deep.

Northernmost Point: Point Barrow, Alaska.

Southernmost Point: Ka Lee (South Cape) — state of Hawaii (Island of Hawaii).

Easternmost Point: West Quoddy Head, Maine.

Westernmost Point: Cape Wrangell, Attu Island (one of the Aleutian Islands), Alaska.

Highest Temperature Ever Recorded: Death Valley, California ❖ 134° F. (Fahrenheit).

Coldest Temperature Ever Recorded: Prospect Creek Camp, Alaska ❖ −79.8° F.

Wettest Place: Mt. Waialeale, Hawaii (on Kauai Island).
   The average annual rainfall is 460 inches.

Strongest Surface Wind Ever Recorded: Mt. Washington, New Hampshire.
   It was blowing 231 miles per hour.

States Surrounded by the Most States: Missouri & Tennessee
   Each is surrounded by eight other states.

United States

Name _____

Date _____

First Native American Settlement:

Nobody knows for certain when the first Native Americans came to the region of today's United States. However, it is known that many different Indian tribes/peoples were living in the region for hundreds, and perhaps thousands, of years before any Europeans ever came to the area. Oraibi, Arizona is most likely the oldest, continuously inhabited Native American settlement in the United States. It was built by the Hopi people in the 1100's.

First Permanent Spanish Settlements:

St. Augustine, Florida, founded in 1565, is considered the first Spanish settle-ment. In 1598, Juan de Oñate founded a Spanish colony at San Juan, New Mexico.

First Permanent British Settlement:

In 1607, about 100 British settlers founded the first permanent British settlement at Jamestown, in today's state of Virginia.

First College: Harvard was founded in 1636.

First Public School:

In 1647, Massachusetts established the first colonial public school.

Independence Declared:

On July 4, 1776, the Colonies adopted the Declaration of Independence and formed the United States of America.

UNITED STATES – State Names

1. Alabama	13. Illinois	25. Missouri	38. Pennsylvania
2. Alaska	14. Indiana	26. Montana	39. Rhode Island
3. Arizona	15. Iowa	27. Nebraska	40. South Carolina
4. Arkansas	16. Kansas	28. Nevada	41. South Dakota
5. California	17. Kentucky	29. New Hampshire	42. Tennessee
6. Colorado	18. Louisiana	30. New Jersey	43. Texas
7. Connecticut	19. Maine	31. New Mexico	44. Utah
8. Delaware	20. Maryland	32. New York	45. Vermont
9. Florida	21. Massachusetts	33. North Carolina	46. Virginia
10. Georgia	22. Michigan	34. North Dakota	47. Washington
11. Hawaii	23. Minnesota	35. Ohio	48. West Virginia
12. Idaho	24. Mississippi	36. Oklahoma	49. Wisconsin
		37. Oregon	50. Wyoming

UNITED STATES – Waterways

Major Rivers

1. Alabama	17. Grand	33. Niobrara	48. Sacramento
2. Allegheny	18. Great Miami	34. North Platte	49. San Joaquin
3. Altamaha	19. Green	35. Nueces	50. San Juan
4. Arkansas	20. Hudson	36. Ohio	51. Savannah
5. Bighorn	21. Humboldt	37. Potomac	52. Snake
6. Brazos	22. Illinois	38. Pearl	53. South Platte
7. Canadian	23. James	39. Pecos	54. Susquehanna
8. Chattahoochee	24. Kanawha	40. Penobscot	55. Tanana
9. Colorado	25. Kansas	41. Platte	56. Tennessee
10. Columbia	26. Kennebec	42. Powder	57. Tombigbee
11. Connecticut	27. Klamath	43. Red River of the North	58. Trinity
12. Cumberland	28. Kuskokwim	44. Republican	59. Wabash
13. Delaware	29. Minnesota	45. Rio Grande	60. White
14. Des Moines	30. Mississippi	46. Roanoke	61. Willamette
15. Flint	31. Missouri	47. Sabine	62. Wisconsin
16. Gila	32. Mohawk		63. Yellowstone
			64. Yukon

Major Lakes

1. Eufaula	17. Tahoe
2. Franklin D. Roosevelt	18. Texoma
3. Francis Case	19. Utah
4. Fort Peck	20. Yellowstone
5. Great Salt Lake	**Surrounding**
6. Keystone	1. Atlantic Ocean
7. Lake of the Ozarks	2. Bering Sea
8. Mead	3. Gulf of Alaska
9. Moosehead	4. Gulf of Mexico
10. Oahe	5. Lake Erie
11. Okeechobee	6. Lake Huron
12. Powell	7. Lake Michigan
13. Pyramid	8. Lake Ontario
14. Sakakawea	9. Lake Superior
15. Salton Sea	10. Pacific Ocean
16. Shasta	11. Puget Sound

U.S. Outline Maps & State Studies: 2

© Golden Educational Center

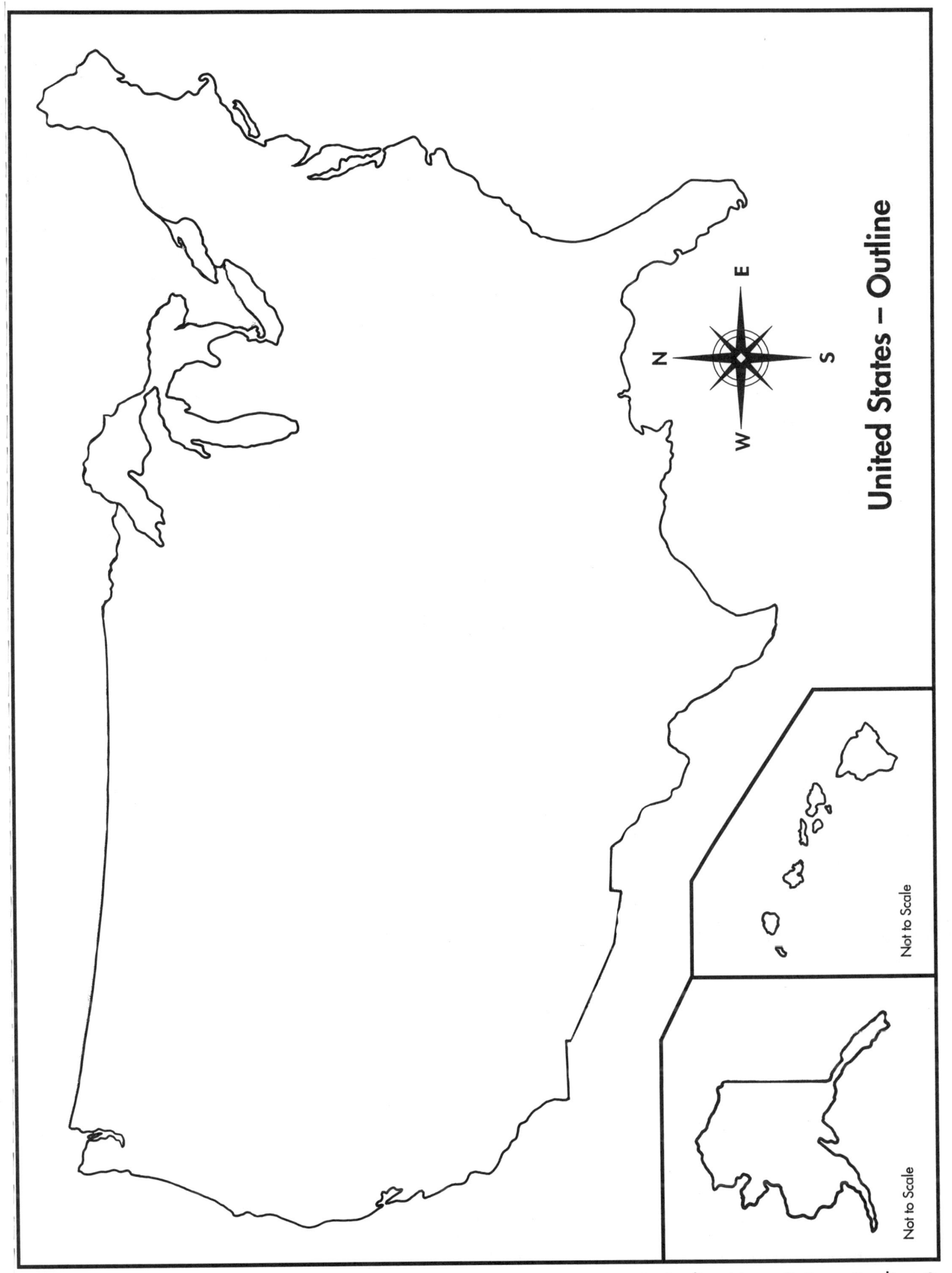

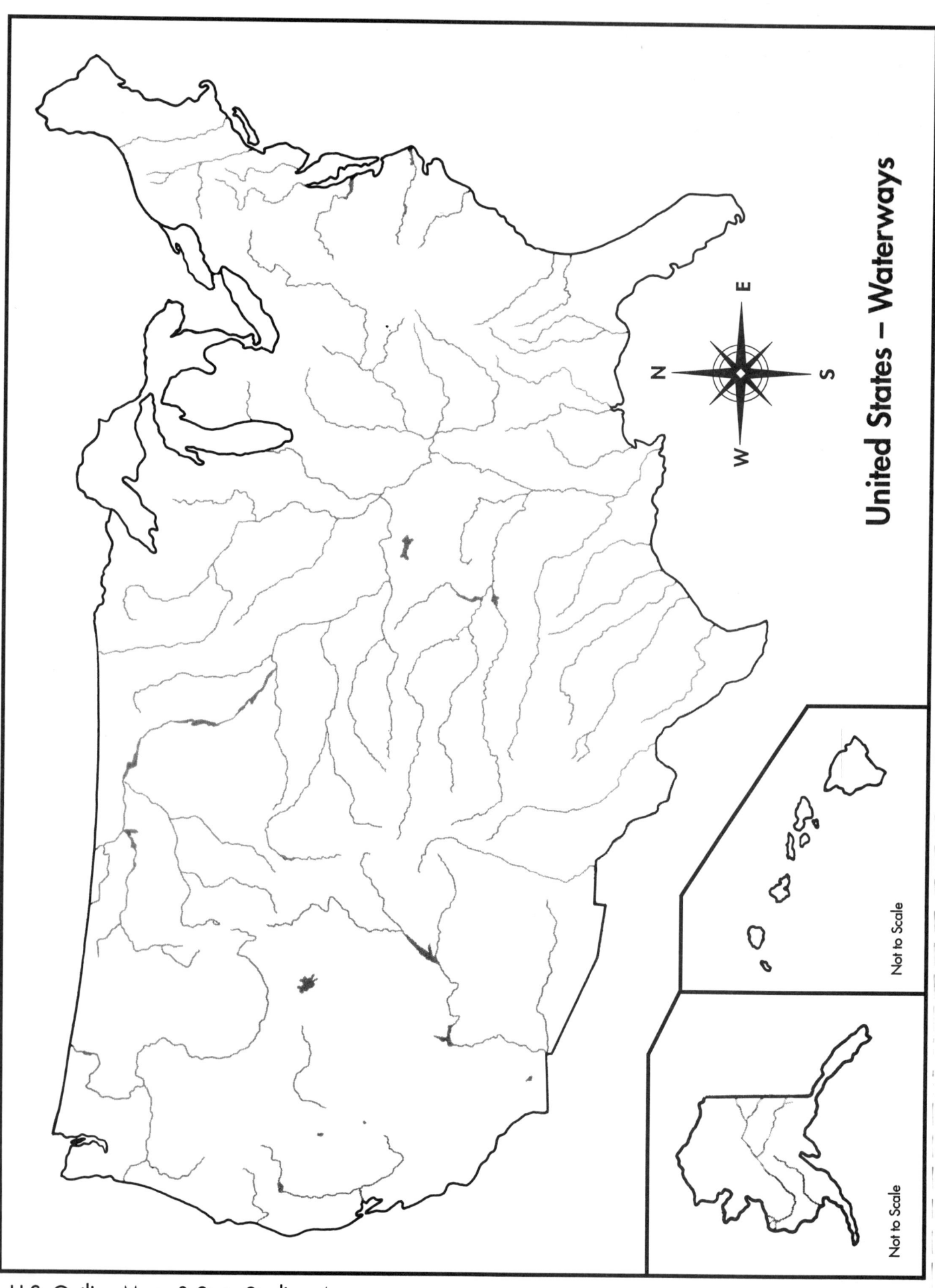

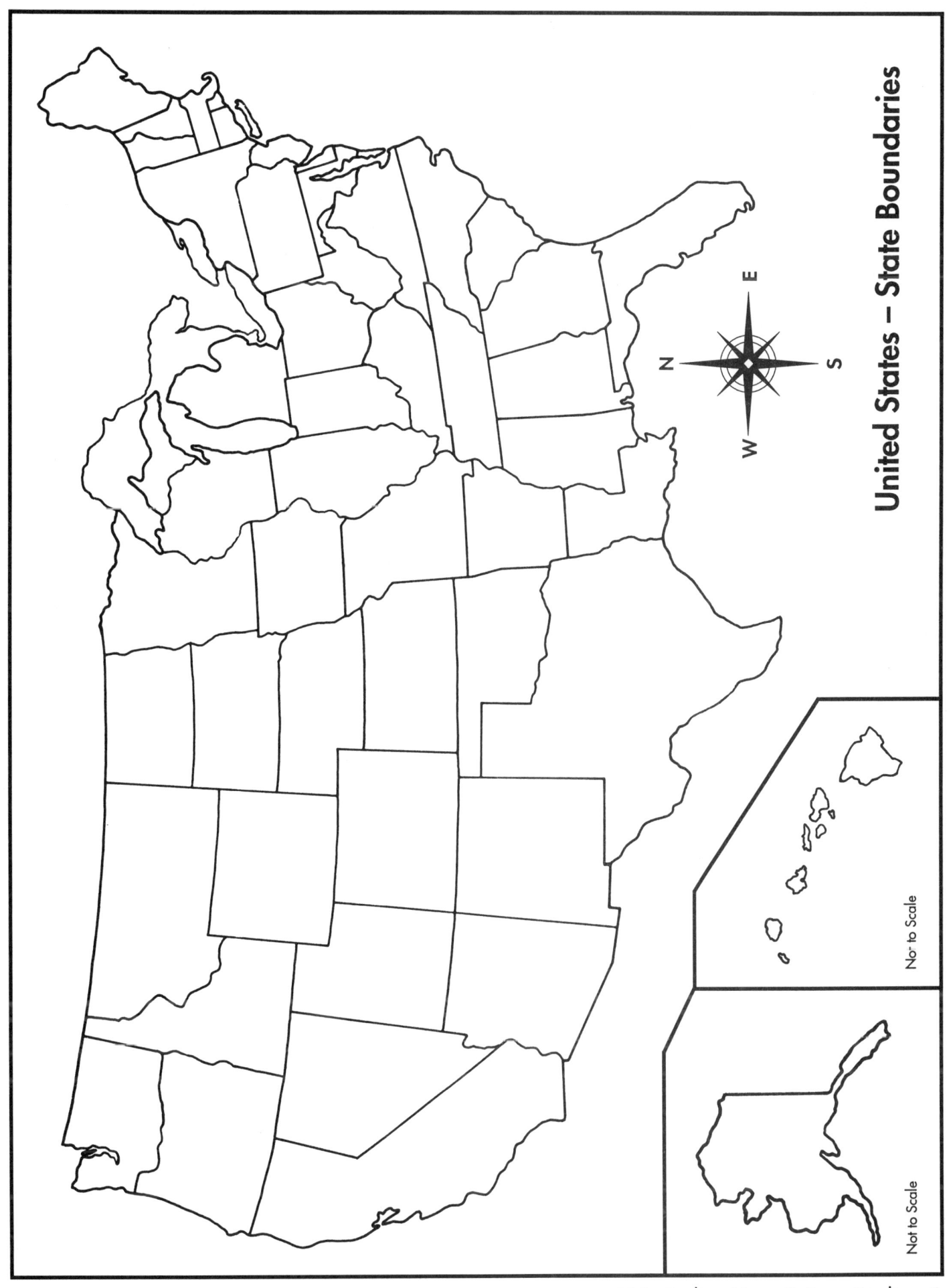

Washington, D.C.

District of Columbia

Name _____

Date _____

First Known Inhabitants:

The first known people to have lived in the Washington area were the Native Americans known as the Piscataway Nation.

First Non-Native American Settlement:

The first white people came to the area to establish farms and plantations in the early 1600's. In 1749, settlers founded Alexandria, the area's first town, in what was then the colony of Virginia.

Established as the Nation's Capital: On December 1, 1800, Washington, D.C. replaced Philadelphia as the capital.

Location: Eastern-Central Coast Region of the United States; bordering the states of Maryland and Virginia.

Area: 68.25 square miles. **Altitude:** *Highest:* 420 feet above sea level. *Lowest:* sea level.

Population (1994 est.): 610,000 people. **Density:** 8791 people per square mile.

Motto: "*Justitia omnibus*" (Justice to all.)

Flower: American Beauty Rose   **Tree:** Scarlet Oak

How Washington, D.C. was Chosen:

During the early years of the United States, several cities served as the nation's capital. In 1783, Congress decided that there should be a permanent center for the government and its agencies. They could not agree on a location. Each state wanted it to be within its own borders. Also, Northerners and Southerners each thought the city should be located in their part of the country.

In 1790, Congress decided to build the capital on land owned by the federal government instead of any state. It agreed to build the city in the South and in return, laws were passed that favored the North.

Congress then decided to build the city along the Potomac River. President George Washington was raised as a child along the river. Because of this, Congress asked him to pick the exact site where the city would be built.

The President made his choice in 1791. It included the land now occupied by Washington, D.C. as well as an additional 30.75 square miles of land west of the Potomac. However, in 1846, Congress returned the additional 30.75 square miles to Virginia. The city's present territory had belonged to Maryland, until it was given to the federal government.

The District of Columbia — also called the City of Washington — was the first carefully planned capital in the world.

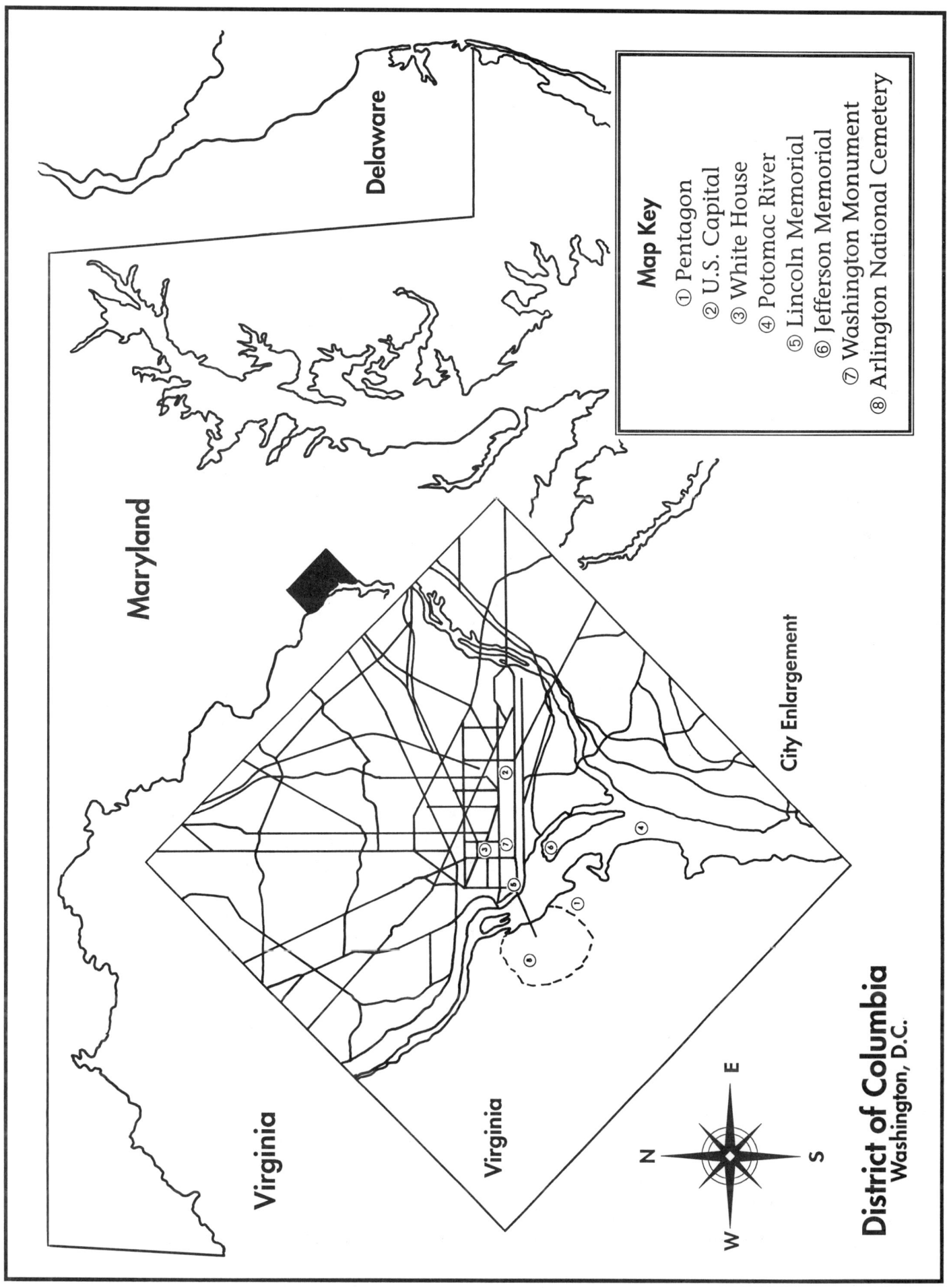

Alabama

The Heart of Dixie ❖ *Yellowhammer State*

Name _____

Date _____

First Non-Native American Settlement:
    In 1702, Fort Louis was founded by two French-Canadian brothers, Jean and Pierre Baptiste Le Moyne. In 1711, the settlement moved 27 miles south to the present site of Mobile.

Organized as a Territory: March 3, 1817.

Admitted to the Union: December 14, 1819 — the 22nd state admitted into the Union.

Location: Southeastern Region of the United States — part of the Southern States.

State Abbreviations: Ala. (traditional use); AL (post office use).

Capital City: Montgomery became the capital city in 1846, after St. Stephens (1817-1819), Huntsville (1819-1820), Cahaba (1820-1826) and Tuscaloosa (1826-1846).

Land Area: 51,705 square miles.   Ranks 28th in size among all of the 50 states. (4th in size among the 14 Southern States.)

Population (1995 approximate): 4,200,000 people. Ranks 22nd among all states.

    Density: 81 people per square mile.
    Distribution: 62% urban (city).   38% rural (non-city).

Largest City: Birmingham — approximate population is 270,000 people.

Highest Elevation: Cheaha Mountain — 2,407 feet above sea level.

State Motto: "Audemus jura nostra defendere." (We dare to defend our rights.)

Important Historical Event: In 1965, Martin Luther King, Jr. led a march from Salem to Montgomery to demonstrate Black people's demands to put an end to discrimination in voter registration, as well as other discriminatory practices.

Alabama's Animals ❖ Plants ❖ Symbols

Game Bird: Wild Turkey	**Bird:** Yellowhammer	**Nut:** Pecan
Horse: Racking	**Salt Water Fish:** Tarpon	**Tree:** Southern Pine
Mineral: Hematite	**Flower:** Camellia	**Rock:** Marble
Fresh Water Fish: Largemouth Bass		**Dance:** Square

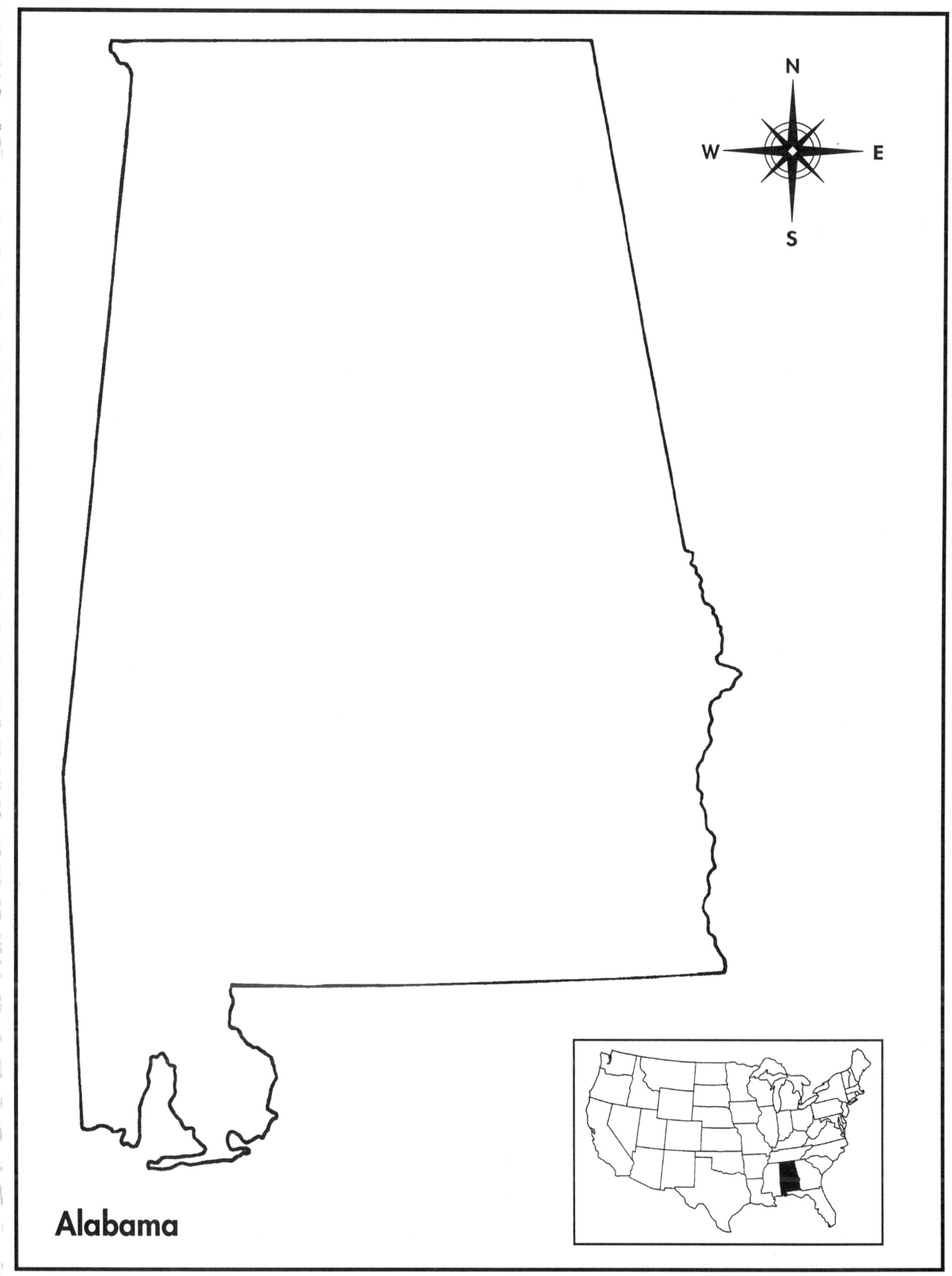

Alabama

U.S. Outline Maps & State Studies: 9

The Last Frontier ❖ *Land of the Midnight Sun*

Name _____

Date _____

First Non-Native American Settlement:
In 1784, Russians established Alaska's first white settlement on Kodiak Island.

Organized as a Territory: 1912.

Admitted to the Union: January 3, 1959 — the 49th state admitted into the Union.

Location: Northwest Region of North America — not part of the contiguous U.S.

State Abbreviations: no traditional use; AK (post office use).

Capital City: Juneau has been the capital since 1900. It was the first capital of the state in 1959. Sitka was the capital from 1884 to 1900.

Land Area: 570,374 square miles. Ranks 1st in size among all of the 50 states. (Alaska is about one-third the size of the entire U.S.)

Population (1995 approximate): 600,000 people. Ranks 49th among all states.

Density: 1 person per square mile.
Distribution: 48% urban (city).   52% rural (non-city).

Largest City: Anchorage — approximate population is 227,000 people.

Highest Elevation: Mt. McKinley — 20,320 feet above sea level.

State Motto: "North to the Future."

Important Historical Event: In 1867, the United States purchased Alaska from Russia for only $7,200,000 — only about 2 cents per acre. At the time of the purchase, many Americans thought Alaska was nothing but a wasteland of ice and snow. The value of the natural resources already taken from Alaska is hundreds of times greater than the original price paid.

Alaska's Animals ❖ Plants ❖ Symbols

Bird: Willow Ptarmigan   **Marine Mammal:** Bowhead Whale   **Gem:** Jade

Mineral: Gold   **Fossil:** Woolly Mammoth   **Fish:** King Salmon

Tree: Sitka Spruce   **Sport:** Dog Mushing   **Flower:** Forget-Me-Not

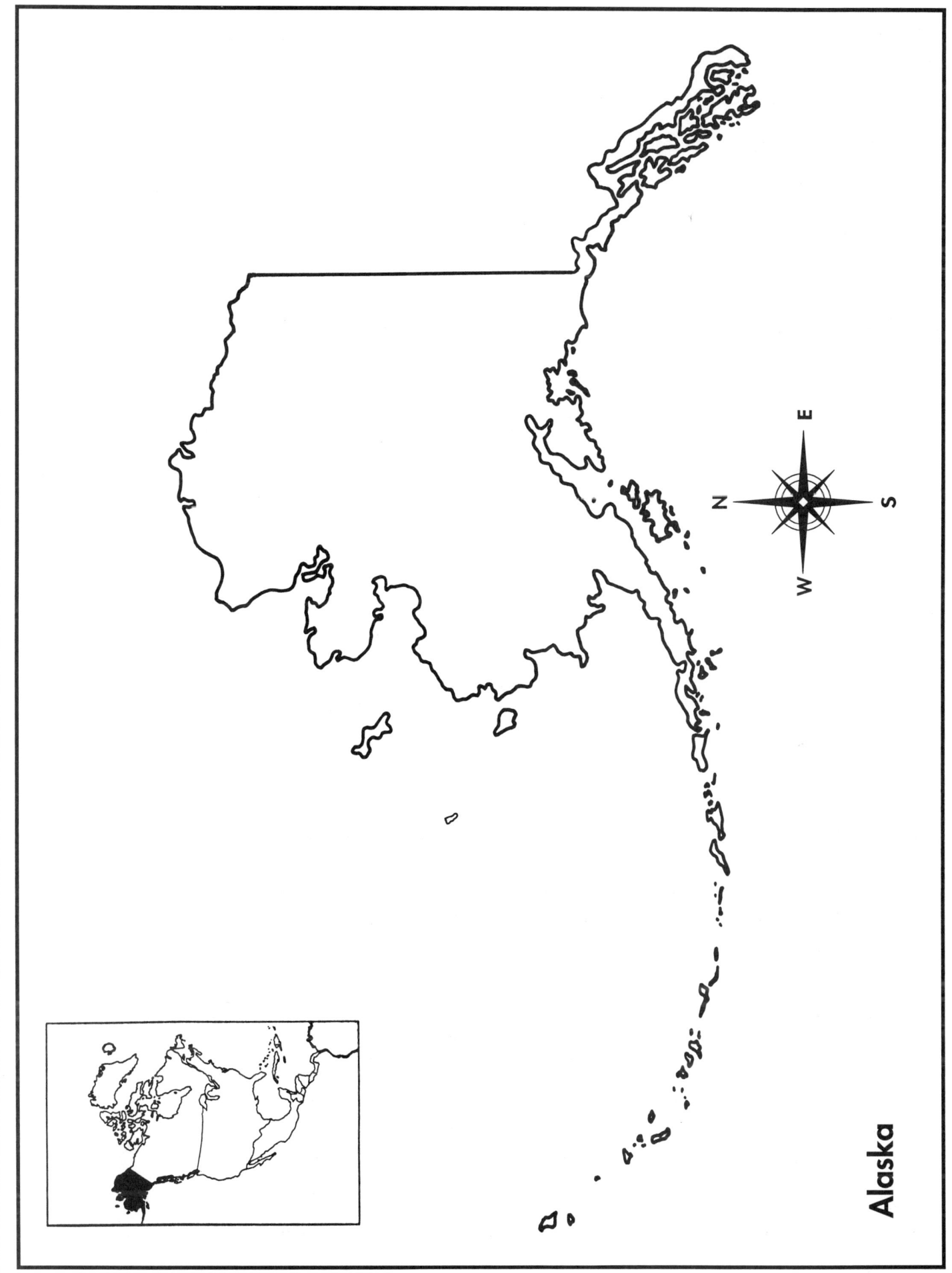

Grand Canyon State

Name _____

Date _____

First Non-Native American Settlement:

In 1752, Spanish troops established the first white settlement, a fort at Tubac. **Note:** Oraibi is probably the oldest continuously inhabited settlement in the United States. It was built by the Hopi Indians during the 1100's.

Organized as a Territory: February 24, 1863.

Admitted to the Union: February 14, 1912 — the 48th state admitted into the Union.

Location: Southwestern Region of the United States — part of the Southwestern States.

State Abbreviations: Ariz. (traditional use); AZ (post office use).

Capital City: Phoenix has been the capital since 1889. Other capitals were Ft. Whipple (1864), Prescott (1864-1867 and 1877-1889) and Tucson (1867-1877).

Land Area: 114,000 square miles. Ranks 6th in size among all of the 50 states. (3rd in size among the 4 Southwestern States.)

Population (1995 approximate): 4,000,000 people. Ranks 23rd among all states.

Density: 34 people per square mile.
Distribution: 80% urban (city).   20% rural (non-city).

Largest City: Phoenix — approximate population is 990,000 people.

Highest Elevation: Humphreys Peak — 12,633 feet above sea level.

State Motto: *"Ditat Deus."* (God Enriches.)

Important Historical Event: In 1969, Navajo Community College at Tsaile, became the first college ever built on an Indian reservation.

Arizona's Animals ❖ Plants ❖ Symbols

Bird: Cactus Wren	**Flower:** Saguaro Cactus	**Tree:** Palo Verde
Colors: Blue & Old Gold	**Mammal:** Ringtail	**Fish:** Arizona Trout
Gemstone: Turquoise	**Neckwear:** Bolo Tie	**Fossil:** Petrified Wood

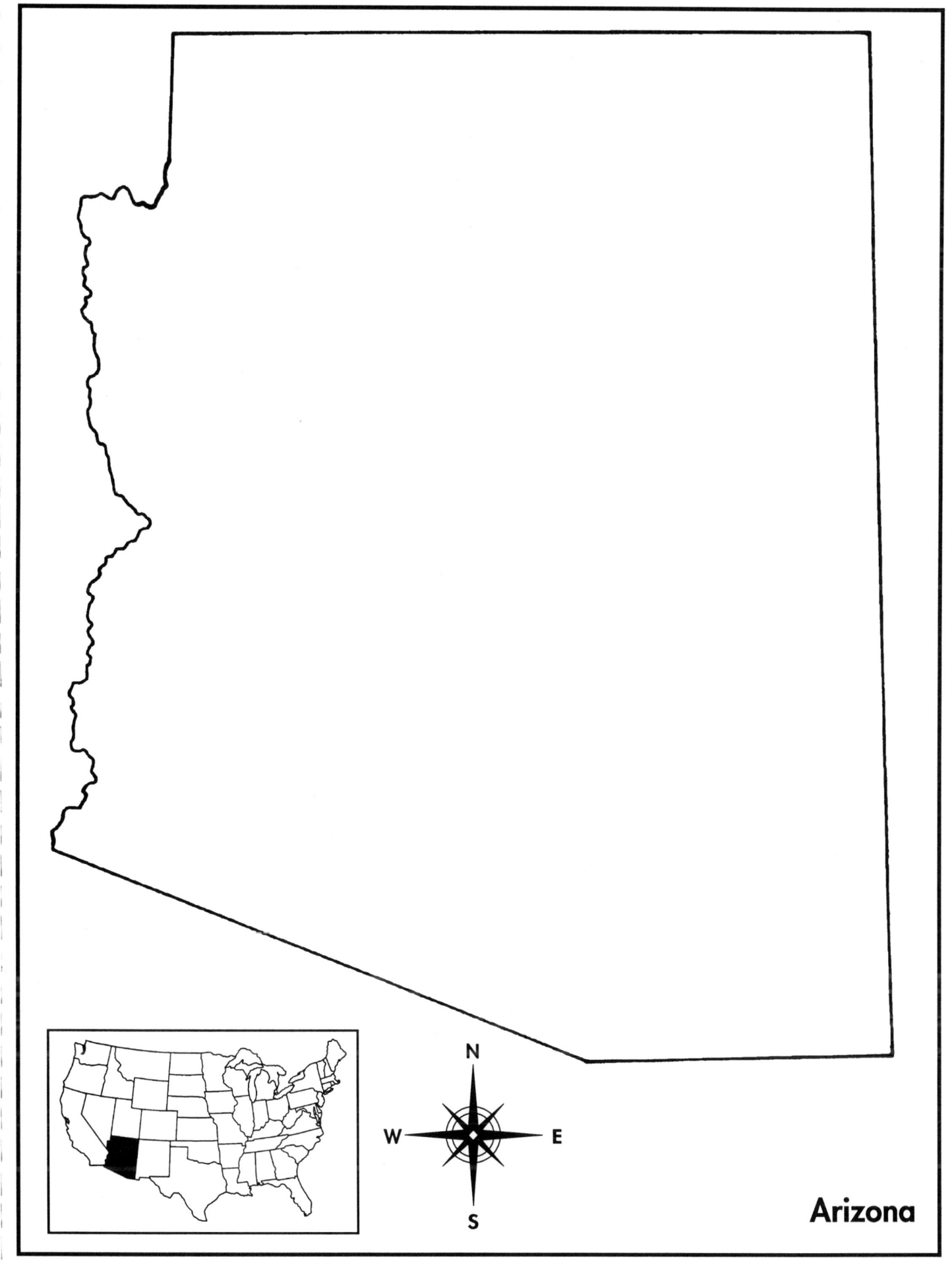

Arkansas

Land of Opportunity

Name _____

Date _____

First Non-Native American Settlement:
　　Arkansas Post was the first permanent white settlement in the state. It grew from a camp that was established by the French explorer, Henry de Tonti in 1686. Arkansas was purchased by the United States from France in the Louisiana Purchase in 1803.

Organized as a Territory: March 2, 1819.

Admitted to the Union: June 15, 1836 — the 25th state admitted into the Union.

Location: South-Central Region of the United States — part of the Southern States.

State Abbreviations: Ark. (traditional use); AR (post office use).

Capital City: Little Rock became the capital city in 1821. Arkansas Post was the capital from 1819 to 1821.

Land Area: 52,075 square miles. Ranks 27th in size among all of the 50 states. (3rd in size among the 14 Southern States.)

Population (1995 approximate): 2,400,000 people. Ranks 33rd among all states.

　　Density: 46 people per square mile.
　　Distribution: 50% urban (city).　　50% rural (non-city).

Largest City: Little Rock — approximate population is 177,000 people.

Highest Elevation: Magazine Mountain — 2,753 feet above sea level.

State Motto: "Regnat Populus." (The people rule.)

Important Historical Event: The only major diamond field in North America lies near Murfreesboro, Arkansas. The first diamonds were found there in 1906.

Arkansas' Animals ❖ Plants ❖ Symbols

Bird: Mockingbird　　　　**Tree:** Pine　　　　**Insect:** Honeybee

Flower: Apple Blossom

U.S. Outline Maps & State Studies: 14　　　　　　　　　　　© Golden Educational Center

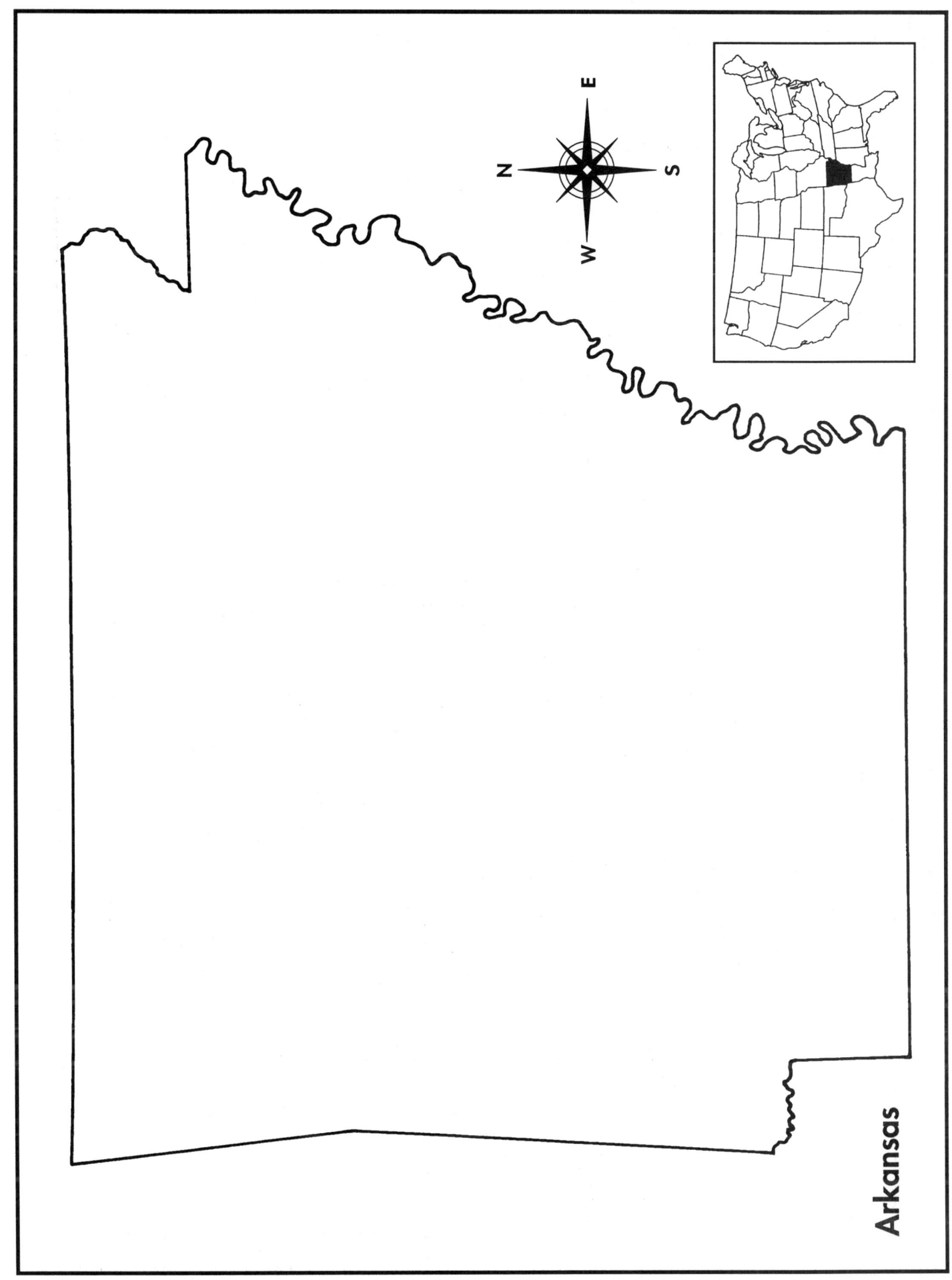

California

The Golden State

Name _____

Date _____

First Non-Native American Settlement:
In 1769, Captain Gaspar de Portolá, governor of Baja (lower) California in Mexico, established the first *"presidio"* (a military fort) where San Diego is today. This was the first permanent settlement on the West Coast.

Organized as a Territory: California was never a territory of the United States.

Admitted to the Union: September 9, 1850 — the 31st state admitted into the Union.

Location: Southwestern Region of the United States — part of the Pacific Coast States.

State Abbreviations: Cal. (traditional use); CA (post office use).

Capital City: Sacramento has been the capital city since 1854. Monterey was the first capital. San Jose, Vallejo, Benicia and San Francisco were also capital cities.

Land Area: 155,973 square miles.   Ranks 3rd in size among all of the 50 states. (1st in size among the 3 Pacific States.)

Population (1995 approximate): 30,500,000 people. Ranks 1st among all states.

Density: 196 people per square mile.
Distribution: 91% urban (city).   9% rural (non-city).

Largest City: Los Angeles — approximate population is 3,500,000 people.

Highest Elevation: Mt. Whitney — 14,494 feet above sea level.

State Motto: *Eureka.* (I have found it.)

Important Historical Event: The Central Pacific Railroad was the first one to cross the Sierra Nevada mountains. Construction of it began in 1864. With the help of mostly Chinese labor, it was completed in 1869. This Transcontinental Railroad linked the Eastern States of the country to the Western States for the first time in history.

California's Animals ❖ Plants ❖ Symbols

Bird: Cal. Valley Quail   **Animal:** Cal. Grizzly Bear

Colors: Blue & Gold   **Fish:** Cal. Golden Trout

Tree: Cal. Redwoods   **Flower:** Golden Poppy

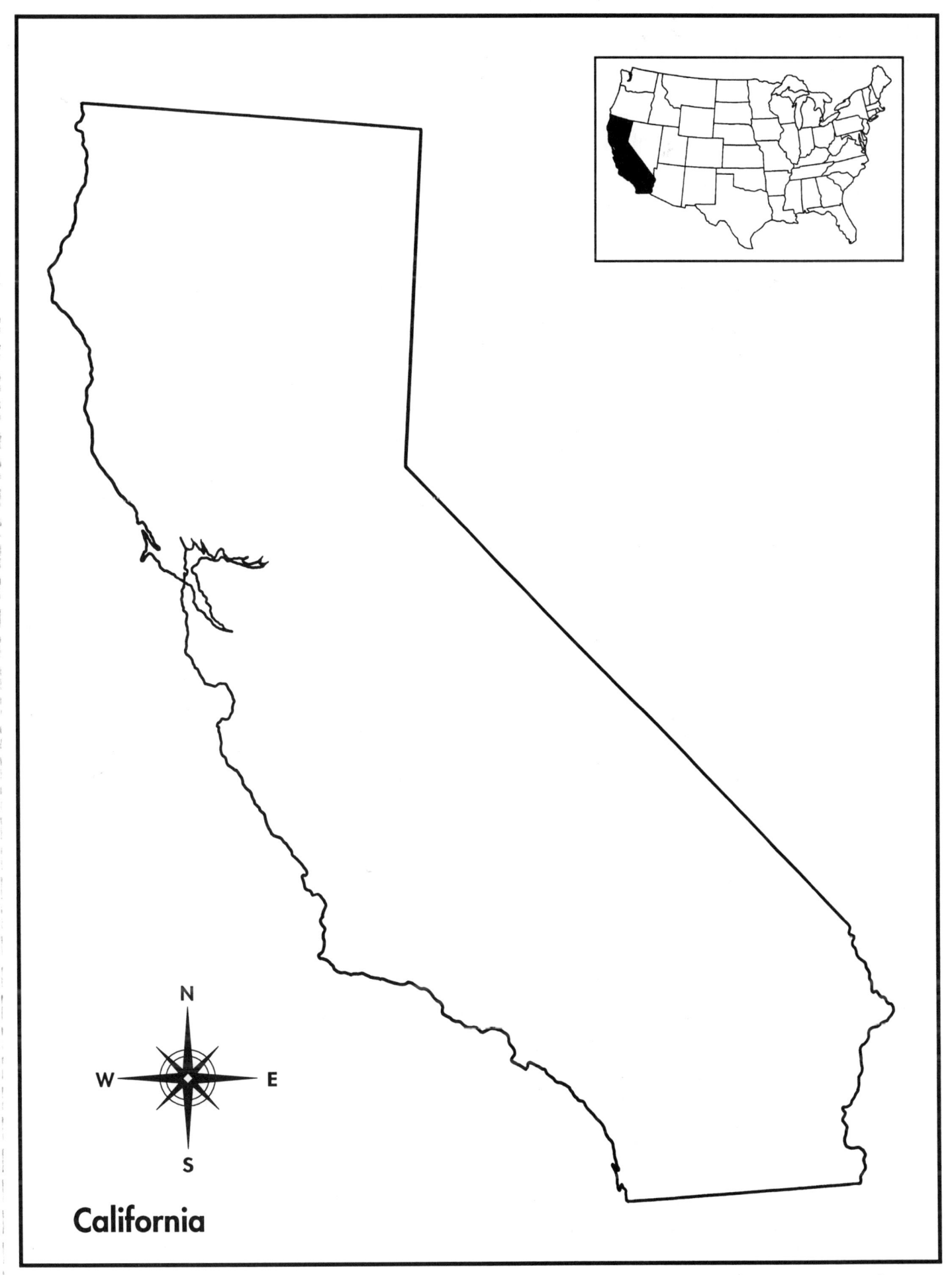

 Colorado

Centennial State

Name _____

Date _____

First Non-Native American Settlement:

   The first permanent American settlement in the region of today's Colorado was Bent's Fort. It was built in 1833, by the Bent and Saint Vrain Fur Company. The fort was near the site of present-day La Junta and used as a base by Kit Carson and other frontiersmen.

Organized as a Territory: February 28, 1861.

Admitted to the Union: August 1, 1876 — the 38th state admitted into the Union.

Location: Western-Central Region of the U.S. — part of the Rocky Mountain States.

State Abbreviations: Colo. (traditional use); CO (post office use).

Capital City: Denver has been the capital city since 1867. The other capitals were Colorado City (now called Colorado Springs) in 1862 and Golden (1862-1867).

Land Area: 103,730 square miles.   Ranks 8th in size among all of the 50 states.
              (3rd in size among the 6 Rocky Mountain States.)

Population (1995 approximate): 3,475,000 people. Ranks 26th among all states.

   Density: 34 people per square mile.
   Distribution: 79% urban (city).   21% rural (non-city).

Largest City: Denver — approximate population is 475,000 people.

Highest Elevation: Mt. Elbert — 14,433 feet above sea level.

State Motto: *"Nil sine Numine."* (Nothing without Providence.)

Important Historical Event: The Alva B. Adams Tunnel was completed in 1947. The Adams Tunnel carries water <u>through</u> the Rocky Mountains to the farmlands in the northeastern part of the state.

Colorado's Animals ❖ Plants ❖ Symbols

Bird: Lark Bunting   **Flower:** Rocky Mt. Columbine

Colors: Blue & White   **Animal:** Rocky Mt. Bighorn Sheep

Gemstone: Aquamarine   **Fossil:** Stegosaurus   **Tree:** Colo. Blue Spruce

---

U.S. Outline Maps & State Studies: 18   © GOLDEN EDUCATIONAL CENTER

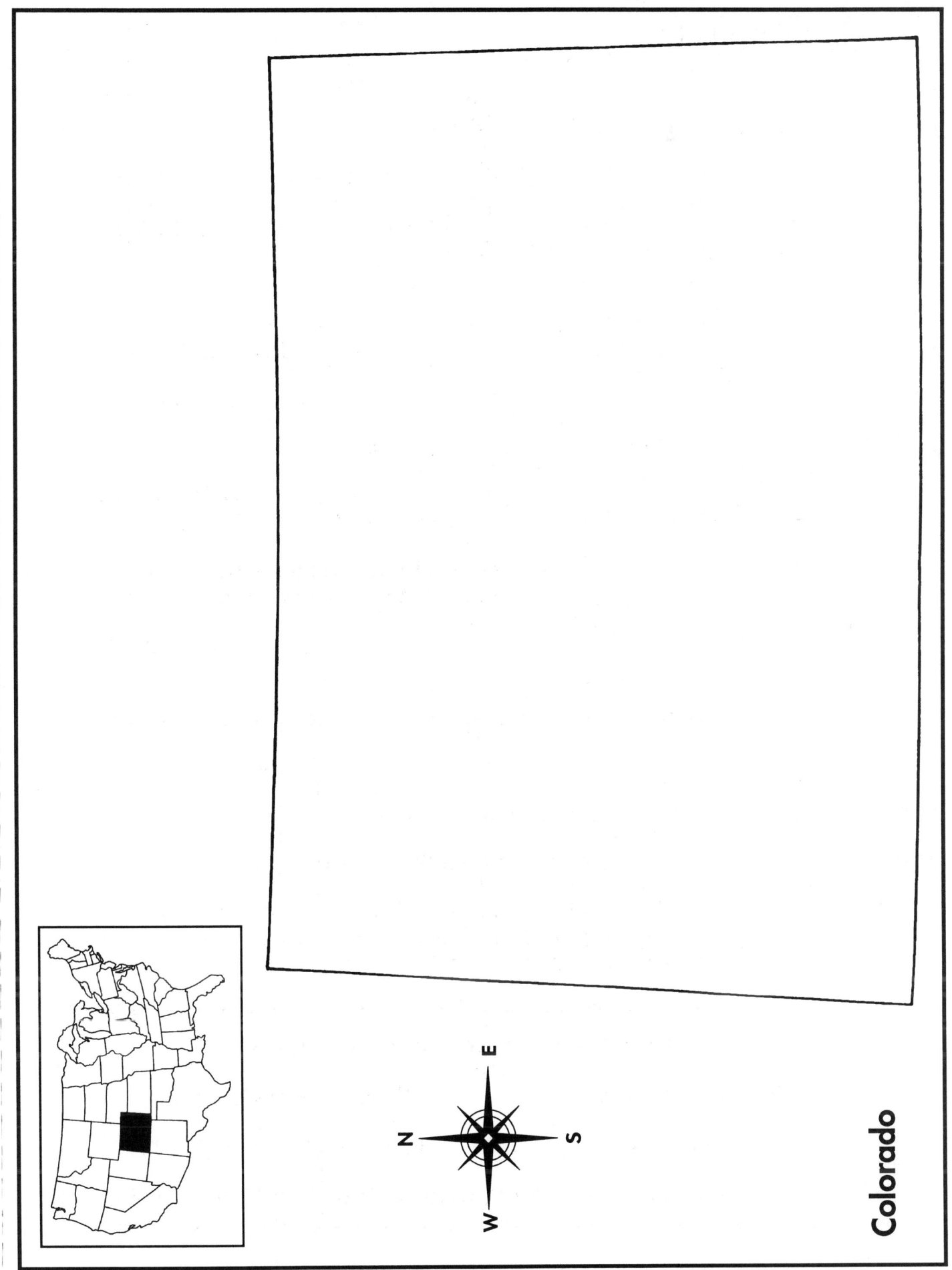

Colorado

U.S. Outline Maps & State Studies: 19

Connecticut

Constitution State ❖ *Nutmeg State*

Name _____

Date _____

First Non-Native American Settlement:
   In 1633, Dutch settlers built a small fort on the present-day site of Hartford. However, they never permanently settled there. Windsor, an English settlement, became the first permanent settlement in Connecticut in 1633.

Organized as a Territory: Connecticut was never a territory of the United States.

Admitted to the Union: January 9, 1788 — the 5th state admitted into the Union.

Location: Northeastern Region of the United States — part of the New England States.

State Abbreviations: Conn. (traditional use); CT (post office use).

Capital City: Hartford became the capital city in 1875. New Haven and Hartford served as twin capitals from 1701 to 1875.

Land Area: 4,845 square miles.   Ranks 48th in size among all of the 50 states. (5th in size among the 6 New England States.)

Population (1995 approximate): 3,285,000 people. Ranks 27th among all states.

   Density: 679 people per square mile.
   Distribution: 77% urban (city).   23% rural (non-city).

Largest City: Bridgeport — approximate population is 142,000 people.

Highest Elevation: South slope of Mt. Frissell — 2,380 feet above sea level.

State Motto: *"Qui transtulit sustinet."* (He who transplanted still sustains.)

Important Historical Event: The first nuclear submarine was built in Groton. It was launched from there in 1965.

Connecticut's Animals ❖ Plants ❖ Symbols

Bird: American Robin   **Flower:** Mt. Laurel   **Tree:** White Oak

Hero: Nathan Hale   **Animal:** Sperm Whale   **Shellfish:** Eastern Oyster

Insect: Praying Mantis   **Mineral:** Garnet   **Ship:** USS Nautilus (SSN571)

U.S. Outline Maps & State Studies: 20   © Golden Educational Center

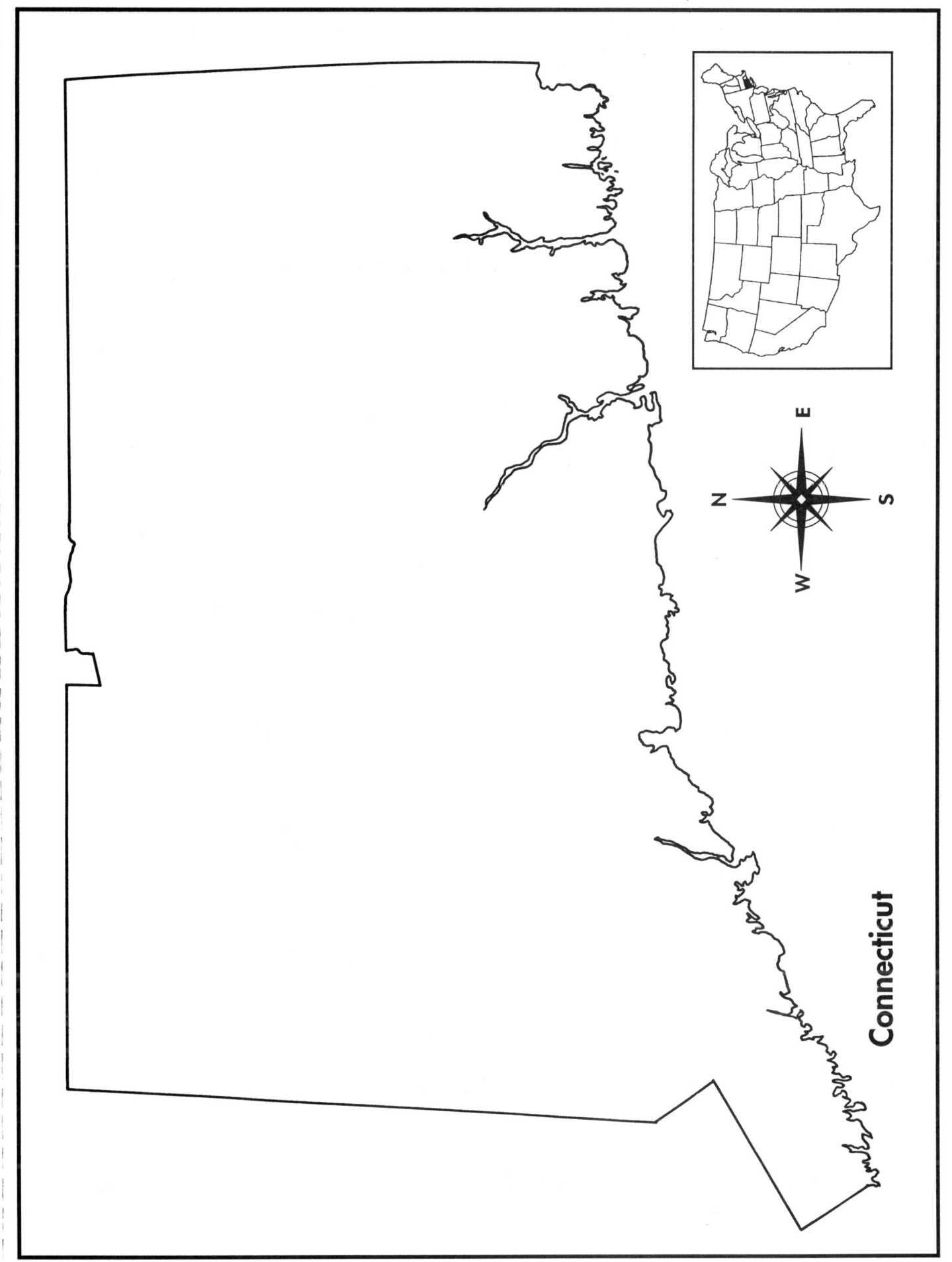

Delaware

The First State ❖ *Diamond State*

Name _____

Date _____

First Non-Native American Settlement:
    The first permanent colony on Delaware soil was New Sweden. It was founded in 1638. The Swedish settlers of this colony built the first log cabins in America.

Organized as a Territory: Delaware was never a territory of the United States.

Admitted to the Union: December 7, 1787 — the 1st state admitted into the Union.

Location: Eastern-Central Coast Region of the U.S. — part of the Southern States.

State Abbreviations: Del. (traditional use); DE (post office use).

Capital City: Dover became the capital city in 1777. New Castle had been the capital since 1704.

Land Area: 1,982 square miles. Ranks 49th in size among all of the 50 states. (14th in size among the 14 Southern States.)

Population (1995 approximate): 690,000 people. Ranks 46th among all states.

    Density: 348 people per square mile.
    Distribution: 72% urban (city).   28% rural (non-city).

Largest City: Wilmington — approximate population is 72,000 people.

Highest Elevation: On Ebright Road in New Castle County — 442 feet above sea level.

State Motto: "Liberty and Independence."

Important Historical Event: Although Delaware is considered a Southern State, it fought on the side of the North in the Civil War (1861 - 1865). The North wanted to do away with slavery while the Southern states wanted slavery to continue the way it had since 1719 — for almost 150 years.

Delaware's Animals ❖ Plants ❖ Symbols

Bird: Blue Hen Chicken   **Flower:** Peach Blossom   **Tree:** American Holly

Insect: Ladybug   **Fish:** Weakfish

Colors: Colonial Blue & Buff

U.S. Outline Maps & State Studies: 22   © golden educational center

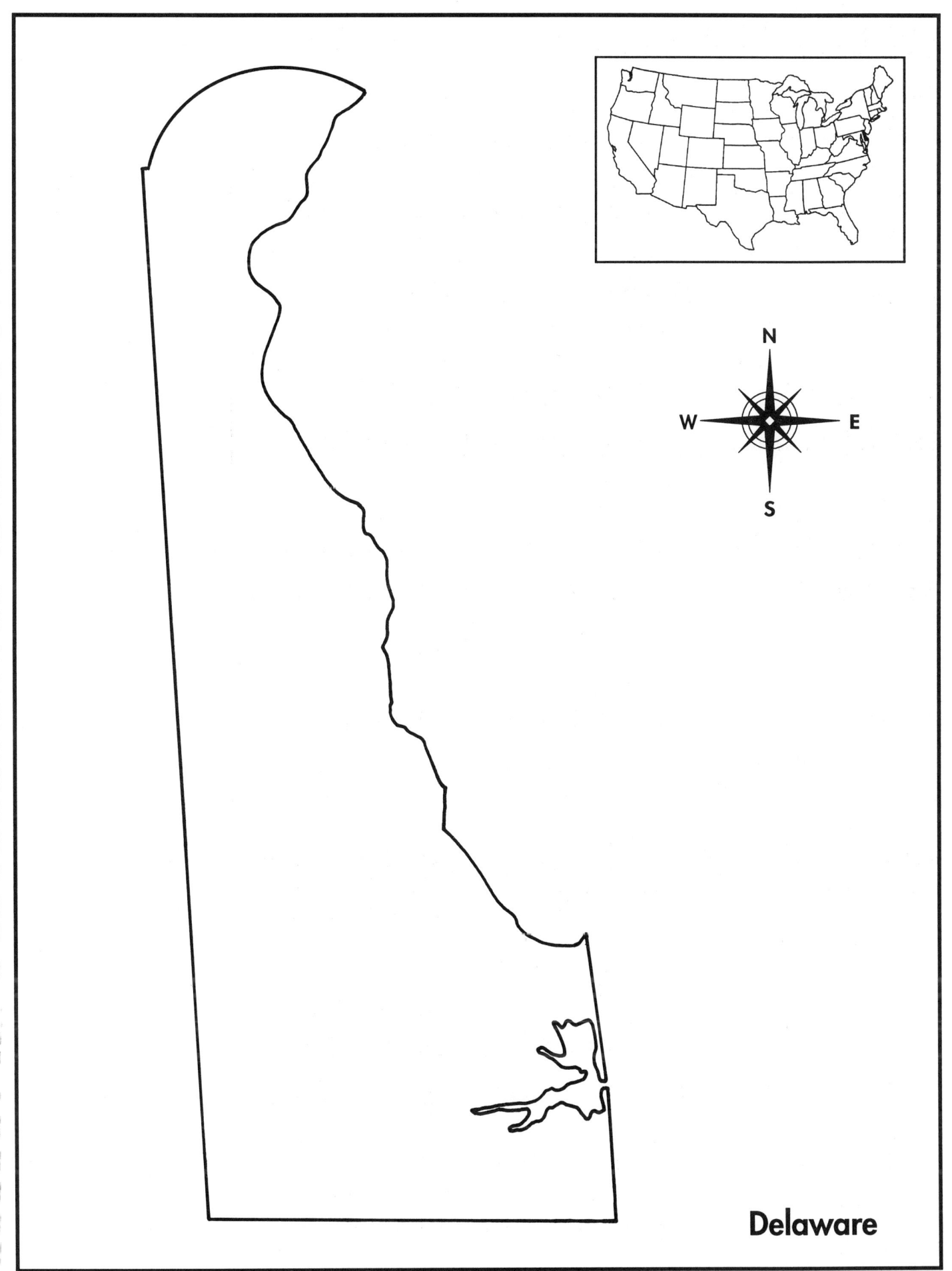

Sunshine State

Name _____

Date _____

First Non-Native American Settlement:
  In 1564, a group of French Protestants established the first white settlement in Florida. They built Fort Caroline near what is now Saint Augustine. (Today's oldest city in the United States.)

Organized as a Territory: March 30, 1822.

Admitted to the Union: March 3, 1845 — the 27th state admitted into the Union.

Location: Southeastern Coast Region of the United States — part of the Southern States.

State Abbreviations: Fla. (traditional use); FL (post office use).

Capital City: Tallahassee became the capital city in 1823, the year after the Territory of Florida was established.

Land Area: 53,997 square miles.   Ranks 26th in size among all of the 50 states. (2nd in size among the 14 Southern States.)

Population (1995 approximate)**:** 13,500,000 people. Ranks 4th among all states.

  Density: 250 people per square mile.
  Distribution: 81% urban (city).   19% rural (non-city).

Largest City: Jacksonville — approximate population is 675,000 people.

Highest Elevation: Walton County — 345 feet above sea level.

State Motto: "In God We Trust."

Important Historical Event: On July 16, 1969, *Apollo 11* was launched from Cape Canaveral (then called Cape Kennedy). This was the first spacecraft to land men on the moon.

Florida's Animals ❖ Plants ❖ Symbols

Tree: Sabal Palmetto Palm

Bird: Mockingbird   **Flower:** Orange Blossom

Song: *"Old Folks at Home"* *(Way Down Upon the Suwannee River)*

U.S. Outline Maps & State Studies: 24

© Golden Educational Center

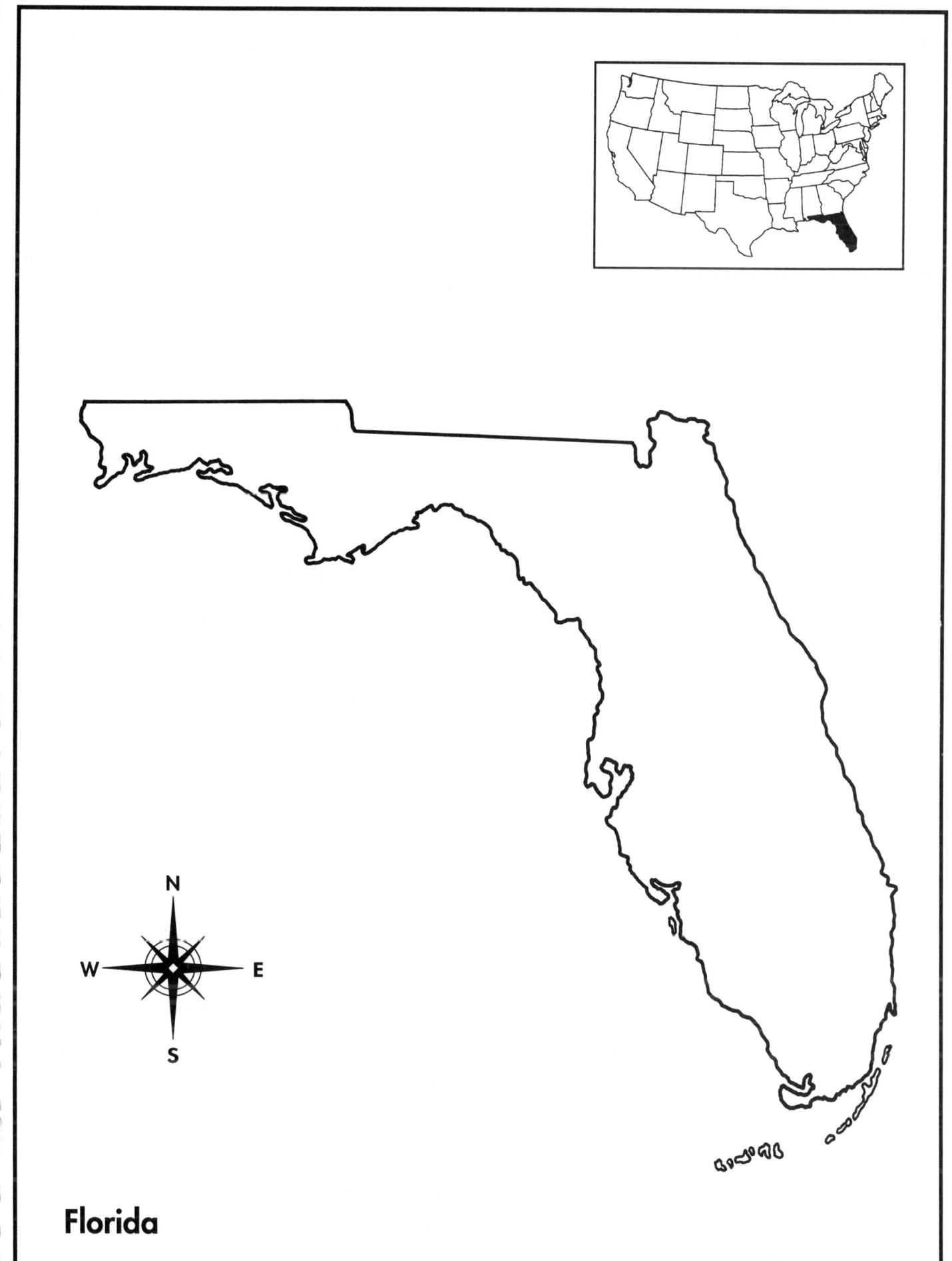

Georgia

Empire State of the South ❖ *Peach State*

Name _____

Date _____

First Non-Native American Settlement:
    Georgia's first permanent white settlement was founded in 1733, at Savannah by James Oglethorpe, a member of the British Parliament (Government).

Organized as a Territory: Georgia was never a territory of the United States.

Admitted to the Union: January 2, 1788 — the 4th state admitted into the Union.

Location: Southeastern Coast Region of the United States — part of the Southern States.

State Abbreviations: Ga. (traditional use); GA (post office use).

Capital City: Atlanta became the capital city in 1868. Earlier capitals were Savannah (1733-1786), Augusta (1786-1795), Louisville (1796-1806) and Milledgeville (1807-1868).

Land Area: 58,919 square miles. Ranks 21st in size among all of the 50 states. (1st in size among the 14 Southern States.)

Population (1995 approximate): 6,760,000 people. Ranks 11th among all states.

    Density: 117 people per square mile.
    Distribution: 60% urban (city).   40% rural (non-city).

Largest City: Atlanta — approximate population is 400,000 people.

Highest Elevation: Brasstown Bald Mountain — 4,784 feet above sea level.

State Motto: "Wisdom, Justice & Moderation."

Important Historical Events: (a.) In 1943, Georgia became the first state to allow 18 year-old people the right to vote. (b.) In 1973, Maynard H. Jackson, Jr., was elected mayor of Atlanta. He was the first Black mayor of a large Southern city.

Georgia's Animals ❖ Plants ❖ Symbols

Tree: Live Oak

Bird: Brown Thrasher   **Flower:** Cherokee Rose

Song: "Georgia on My Mind"

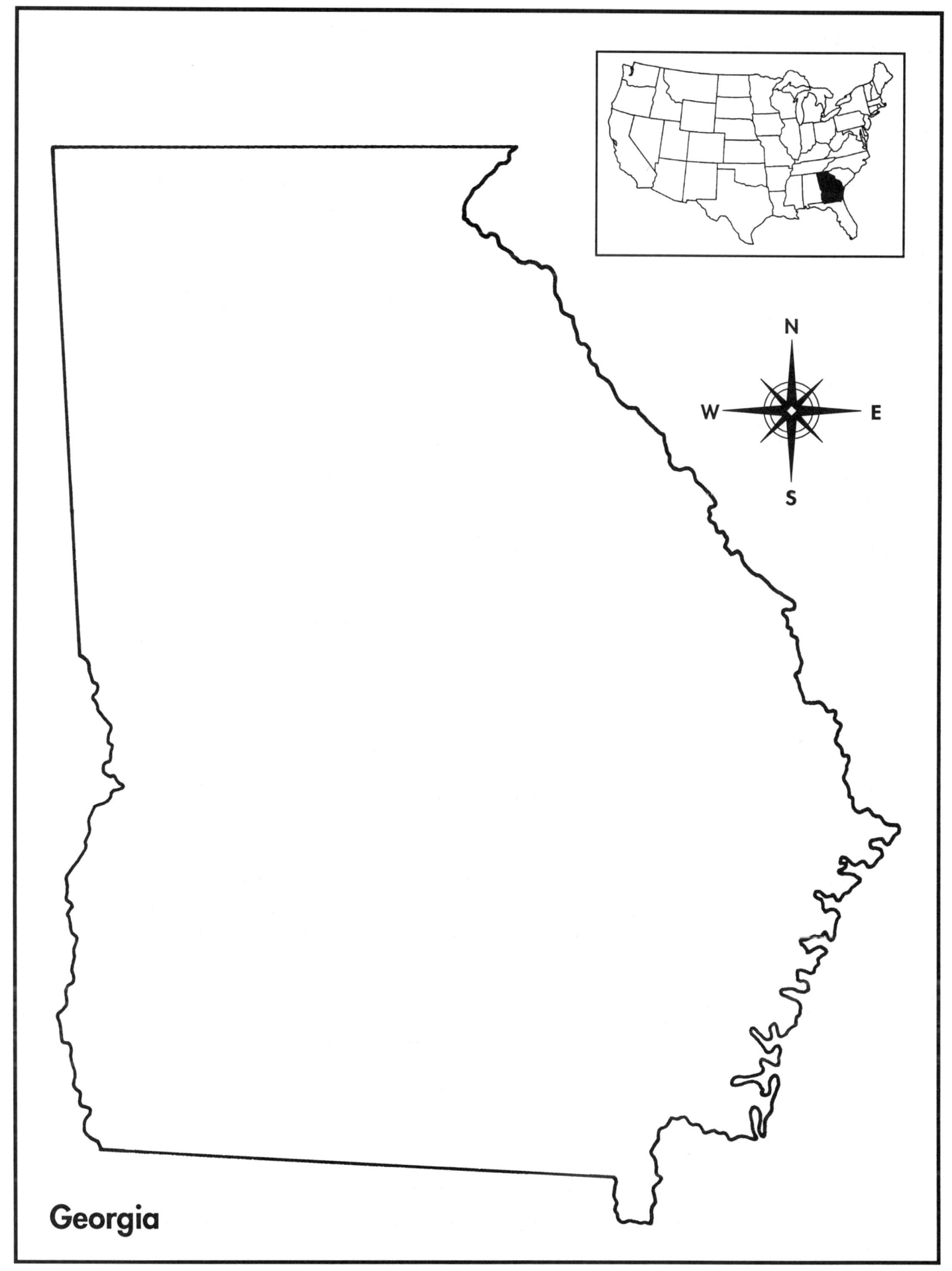

Aloha State

Name _____

Date _____

First Non-Polynesian Settlement:
   Polynesians were the first people to settle on the islands about 2,000 years ago. In 1813, Don Francisco de Paula Marín, a Spanish settler, wrote of planting pineapples. This may have been the the first non-Polynesian settlement; however, it is not certain.

Organized as a Territory: 1900.

Admitted to the Union: August 21, 1959 — the 50th state admitted into the Union.

Location: Mid-Pacific Ocean — not part of the Contiguous U.S. or No. American mainland.

State Abbreviations: no traditional use; HI (post office use).

Capital City: Honolulu has been the capital city since Hawaii was admitted into the Union.

Land Area: 6,423 square miles.   Ranks 47th in size among all of the 50 states.
   (Hawaii is the only state that is entirely made up of islands — 132 in all.)

Population (1995 approximate): 1,170,000 people.   Ranks 40th among all states.

   Density: 182 people per square mile.
   Distribution: 83% urban (city).   17% rural (non-city).

Largest City: Honolulu — approximate population is 380,000 people.

Highest Elevation: Mauna Kea — 13,796 feet above sea level.

State Motto: "The life of the land is perpetuated in righteousness."

Important Historical Events: (a.) In 1927, A.F. Hegenberger and L.J. Maitland made the first airplane flight from the United States mainland to the Hawaiian Islands. (b.) Pearl Harbor (an inlet on the south coast of the island of Oahu near Honolulu: site of a U.S. Naval base) was bombed by Japanese fighter planes on December 7, 1941. This attack led the U.S. to declare war on the Japanese government in World War II.

Hawaii's Animals ❖ Plants ❖ Symbols

Tree: Kukui (Candlenut)

Bird: Nene (Hawaiian Goose)   **Flower:** Yellow Hibiscus

Song: "Hawaii Ponoi"

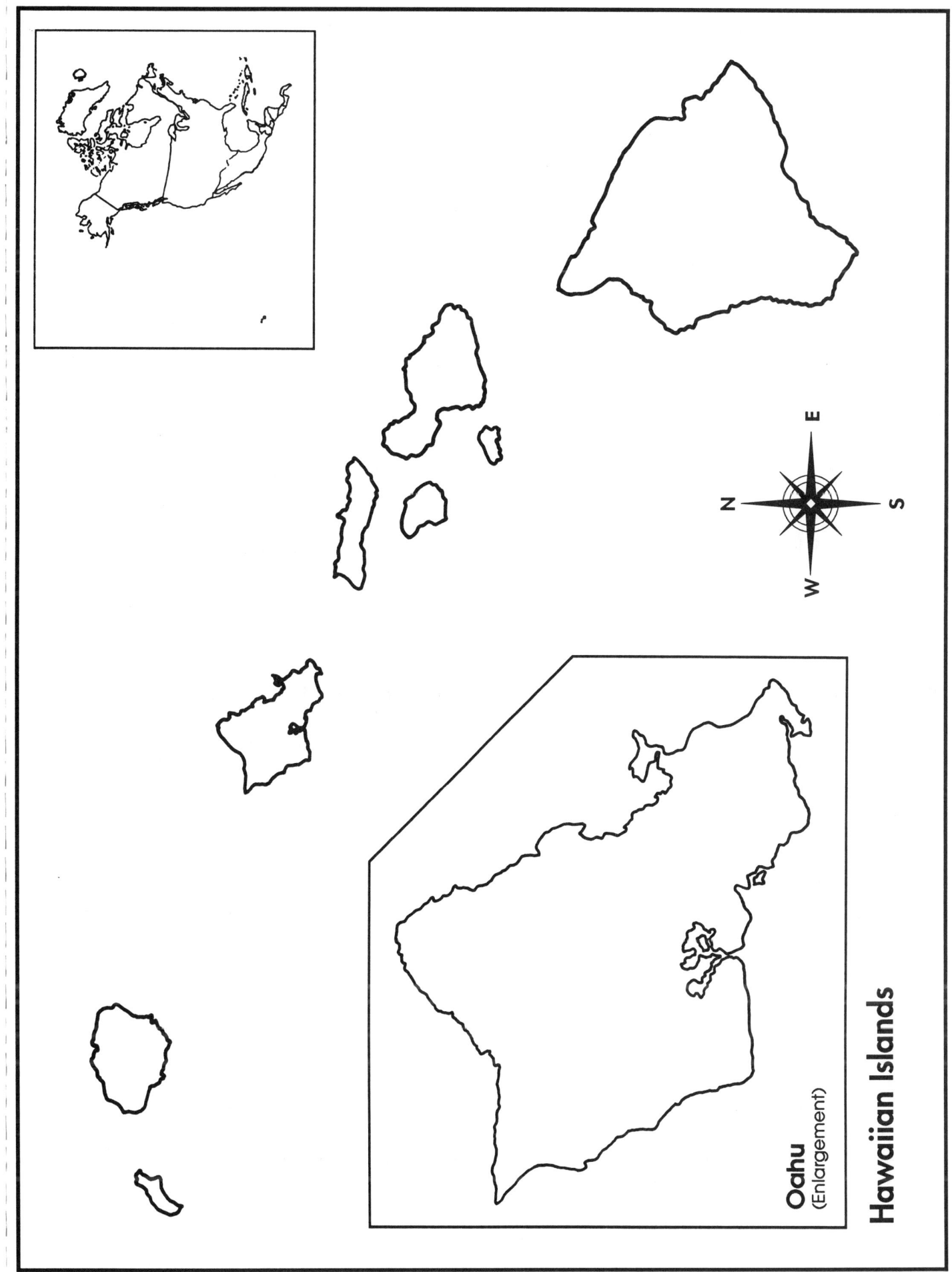

Idaho

Gem State ❖ *Spud State* ❖ *Panhandle State*

Name _____

Date _____

First Non-Native American Settlement:
 David Thompson, a Canadian explorer, built a fur-trading post on the shores of Pend Oreille Lake in 1809. Cataldo Mission is the oldest building still standing in Idaho.

Organized as a Territory: March 3, 1863.

Admitted to the Union: July 3, 1890 — the 43rd state admitted into the Union.

Location: Northwestern Region of the United States — part of the Rocky Mountain States.

State Abbreviations: Ida. (traditional use); ID (post office use).

Capital City: Boise has been the capital city since 1864. Lewiston was the capital from 1863 to 1864.

Land Area: 82,751 square miles.   Ranks 11th in size among all of the 50 states. (5th in size among the 6 Rocky Mountain States.)

Population (1995 approximate): 1,075,000 people. Ranks 42nd among all states.

 Density: 13 people per square mile.
 Distribution: 54% urban (city).   46% rural (non-city).

Largest City: Boise — approximate population is 130,000 people.

Highest Elevation: Borah Peak — 12,662 feet above sea level.

State Motto: "*Esto Perpetua.*" (It is forever.)

Important Historical Event: In 1951, electricity was generated from nuclear energy for the first time. This event took place at a reactor testing station near Idaho Falls.

Idaho's Animals ❖ Plants ❖ Symbols

Bird: Mountain Bluebird   **Flower:** Syringa

Horse: Appaloosa   **Folk Dance:** Square Dance   **Tree:** White Pine

Gem: Star Garnet   **Fossil:** Hagerman Horse

U.S. Outline Maps & State Studies: 30   © GOLDEN EDUCATIONAL CENTER

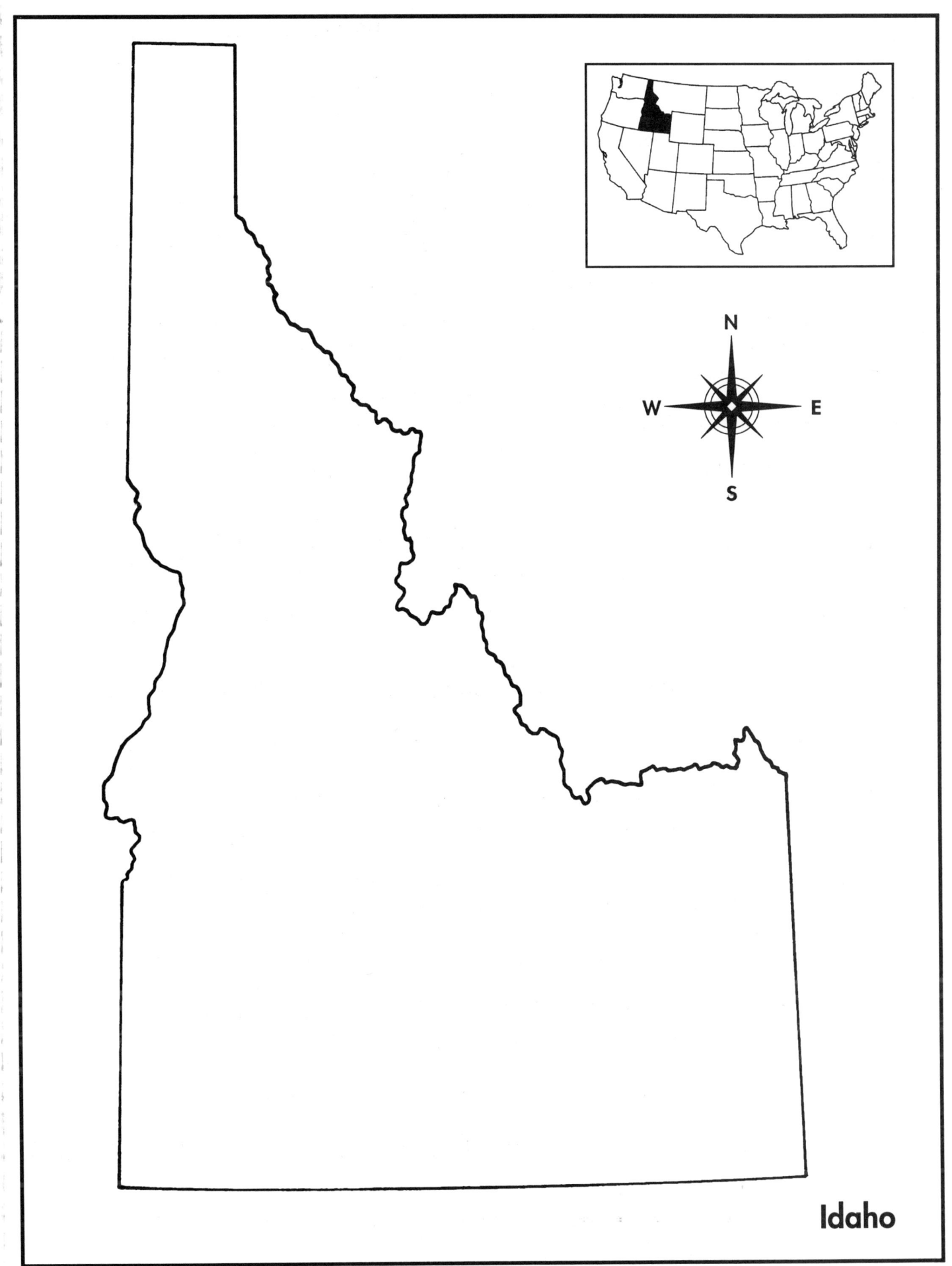

Idaho

U.S. Outline Maps & State Studies: 31

Prairie State ❖ *Land of Lincoln*

Name _____

Date _____

First Non-Native American Settlement:

   In 1675, Father J. Marquette and Louis Joliet started a mission at the Kaskaskia Indian village near the present site of Utica. In 1699, a different French priest founded a mission and trading post in Cahokia. This was the first permanent town in the Illinois region.

Organized as a Territory: February 3, 1809.

Admitted to the Union: December 3, 1818 — the 21st state admitted into the Union.

Location: Central Region of the United States — part of the Midwestern States.

State Abbreviations: Ill. (traditional use); IL (post office use).

Capital City: Springfield has been the capital city since 1839. Other capital cities were Kaskaskia (1818-1820) and Vandalia (1820-1839).

Land Area: 55,593 square miles.   Ranks 24th in size among all of the 50 states. (9th in size among the 12 Midwestern States.)

Population (1995 approximate): 11,800,000 people. Ranks 6th among all states.

   Density: 212 people per square mile.
   Distribution: 83% urban (city).   17% rural (non-city).

Largest City: Chicago — approximate population is 2,800,000 people.

Highest Elevation: Charles Mound (a reactor testing station) — 1,235 feet above sea level.

State Motto: "State Sovereignty, National Union."

Important Historical Event: The University of Chicago is considered the *Birthplace of Atomic Energy*.

Illinois' Animals ❖ Plants ❖ Symbols

Bird: Cardinal   **Tree:** White Oak

Flower: Violet   **Animal:** White-tailed Deer   **Fish:** Bluegill

Mineral: Fluorite   **Insect:** Monarch Butterfly

U.S. Outline Maps & State Studies: 32   © GOLDEN EDUCATIONAL CENTER

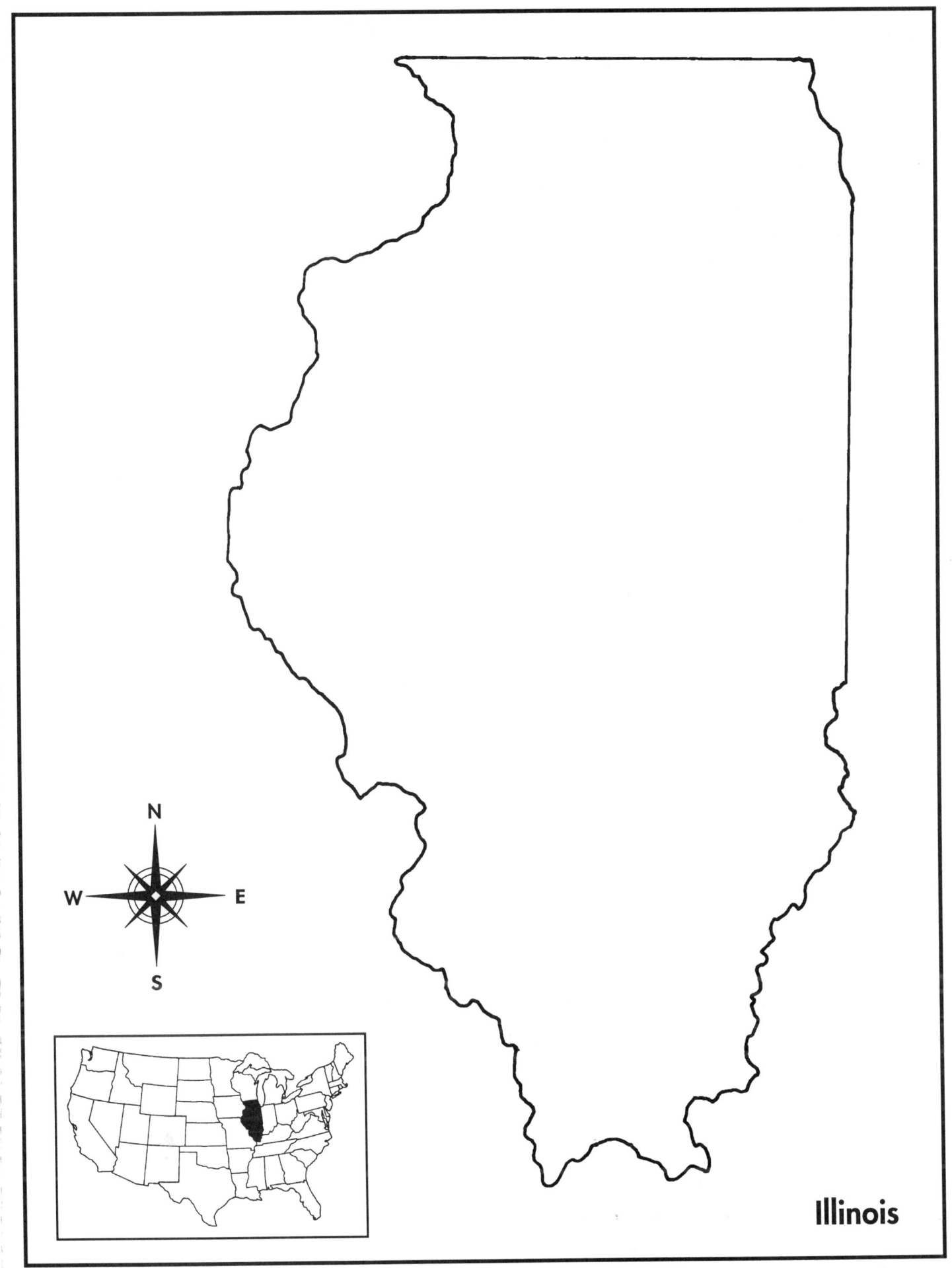

Hoosier State

Name _____

Date _____

First Non-Native American Settlement:
    Vincennes was the first permanent settlement in the Indiana region. The English founded it about 1731. George Rogers Clark and his group of frontiersmen captured it from the English on February 24, 1799.

Organized as a Territory: May 7, 1800.

Admitted to the Union: December 11, 1816 — the 19th state admitted into the Union.

Location: Central Region of the United States — part of the Midwestern States.

State Abbreviations: Ind. (traditional use); IN (post office use).

Capital City: Indianapolis has been the capital city since 1825. Other capital cities were Vincennes (1800-1813) and Corydon (1813-1824).

Land Area: 35,870 square miles. Ranks 38th in size among all of the 50 states. (12th in size among the 12 Midwestern States.)

Population (1995 approximate)**:** 5,700,000 people. Ranks 14th among all states.

    Density: 159 people per square mile.
    Distribution: 83% urban (city).   17% rural (non-city).

Largest City: Indianapolis — approximate population is 750,000 people.

Highest Elevation: Wayne County — 1,257 feet above sea level.

State Motto: "The Crossroads of America."

Important Historical Events: (a.) In 1889, Elwood Hayes built one of the first successful gas-powered automobiles in Kokomo. (b.) The first 500-mile Memorial Day automobile race was held in Indianapolis. It is today's "Indy 500 Race."

Indiana's Animals ❖ Plants ❖ Symbols

Bird: Cardinal   **Flower:** Peony   **Tree:** Tulip Poplar

Song: "On the Banks of the Wabash, Far Away"

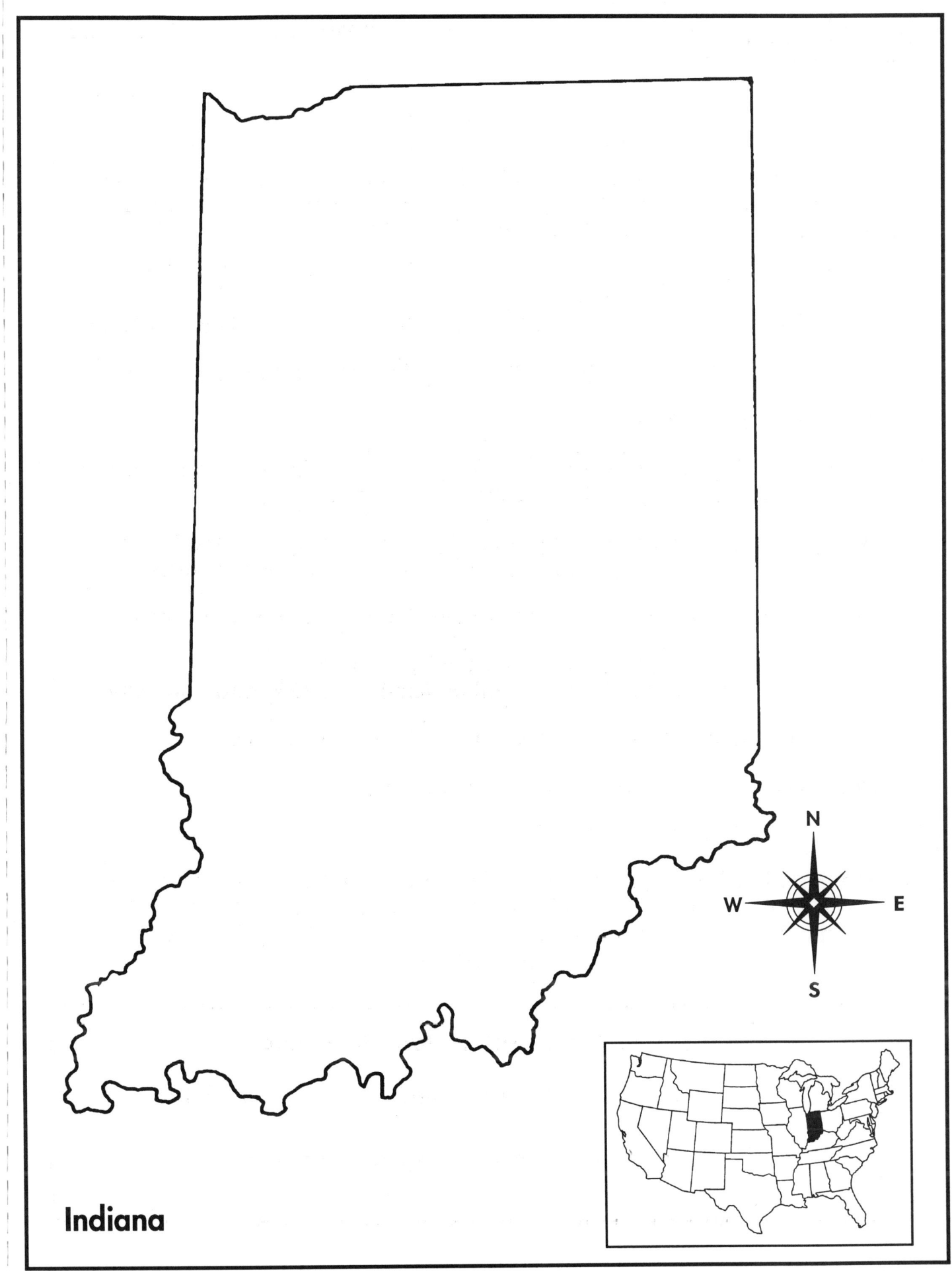

Iowa
Hawkeye State

Name _____

Date _____

First Non-Native American Settlement:
    Julien Dubuque got permission from the Fox Indians in 1788 to mine lead near present-day Dubuque. He was Iowa's first settler. Several other trappers and hunters soon came after Dubuque.

Organized as a Territory: June 12, 1838.

Admitted to the Union: December 28, 1846 — the 29th state admitted into the Union.

Location: North-Central Region of the United States — part of the Midwestern States.

State Abbreviations: Ia. (traditional use); IA (post office use).

Capital City: Des Moines has been the capital since 1857. Other capital cities were Burlington (1838-1841) and Iowa City (1841-1857).

Land Area: 55,875 square miles. Ranks 23rd in size among all of the 50 states. (8th in size among the 12 Midwestern States.)

Population (1995 approximate): 2,850,000 people. Ranks 30th among all states.

    Density: 51 people per square mile.
    Distribution: 59% urban (city).   41% rural (non-city).

Largest City: Des Moines — approximate population is 200,000 people.

Highest Elevation: North boundary of Osceola County — 1,670 feet above sea level.

State Motto: "Our liberties we prize and our rights we will maintain."

Important Historical Event: Most Iowa farmers lost their land because they could not make the payments to the banks (1920's - 1930's). In the 1940's they regained their prosperity.

Iowa's Animals ❖ Plants ❖ Symbols

Bird: Eastern Goldfinch   **Flower:** Wild Rose

Colors: Red, White & Blue (In Iowa's Flag)

Tree: Oak   **Rock:** Geode

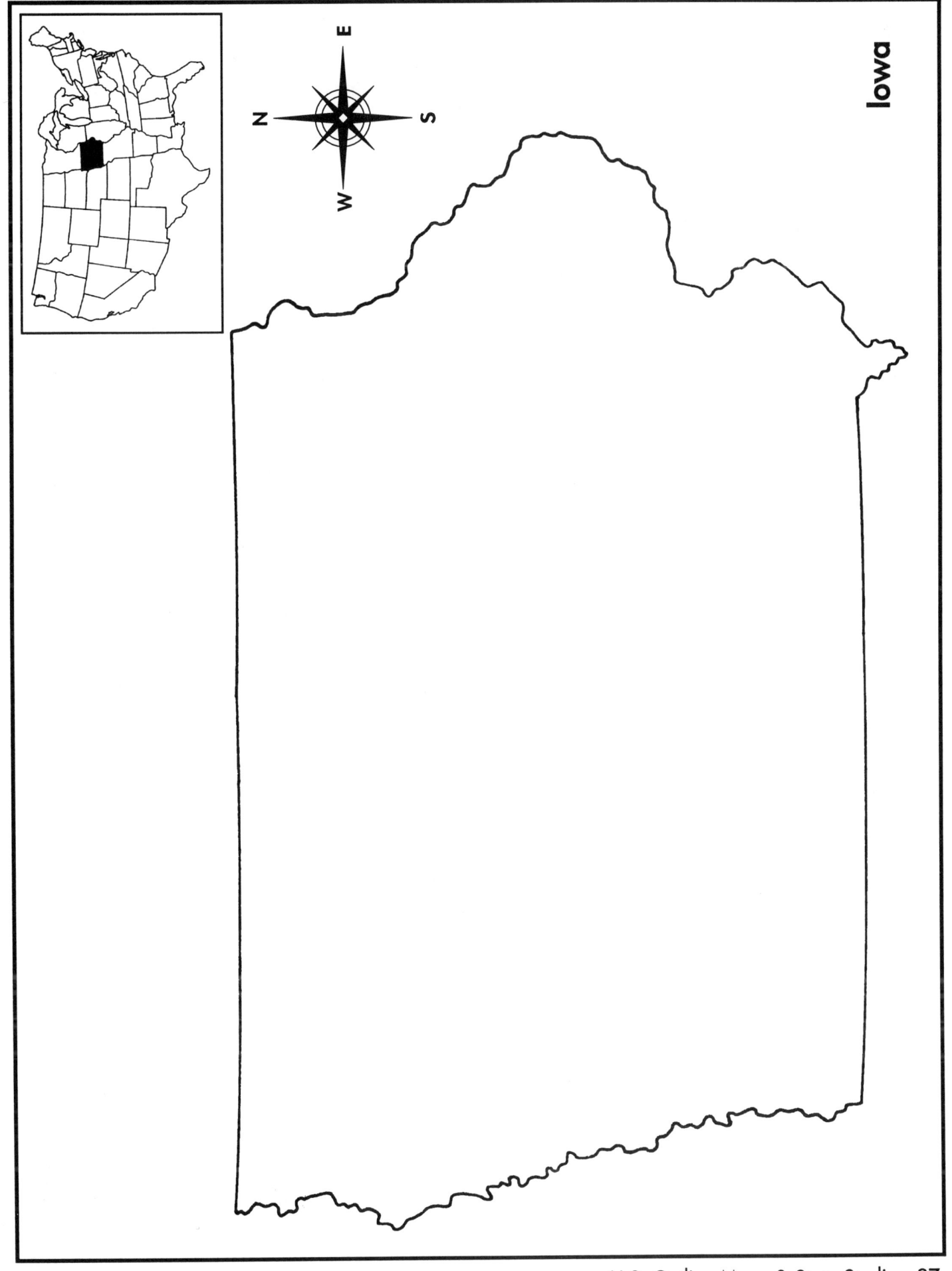

Sunflower State ❖ Jayhawk State

Name _____

Date _____

First Non-Native American Settlement:
   Captain Henry Leavenworth established the first permanent white settlement in Kansas where present-day Fort Leavenworth is located. The settlement was founded in 1827, in order to help protect wagon trains using the Santa Fe Trail.

Organized as a Territory: May 30, 1854.

Admitted to the Union: January 29, 1861 — the 34th state admitted into the Union.

Location: Central Region of the United States — part of the Midwestern States.

State Abbreviations: Kans. (traditional use); KS (post office use).

Capital City: Topeka has been the capital city since 1861. Other capital cities were Fort Leavenworth (1854), Shawnee Mission (1854-1855) and Lecompton (1855-1861).

Land Area: 81,823 square miles.   Ranks 13th in size among all of the 50 states. (1st in size among the 12 Midwestern States.)

Population (1995 approximate): 2,600,000 people. Ranks 32nd among all states.

   Density: 32 people per square mile.
   Distribution: 65% urban (city).   35% rural (non-city).

Largest City: Wichita — approximate population is 310,000 people.

Highest Elevation: Mt. Sunflower — 4,039 feet above sea level.

State Motto: "Ad astra per aspera." (To the stars through difficulties.)

Important Historical Event: In the 1870's, Russian settlers in four counties of Kansas planted a new variety of wheat, called *"Red Turkey,"* for the first time. This variety of wheat has helped make Kansas the leading producer of wheat in the United States.

Kansas' Animals ❖ Plants ❖ Symbols

Bird: Western Meadowlark   **Flower:** Sunflower

Animal: Buffalo   **Tree:** Cottonwood

Song: "Home on the Range"

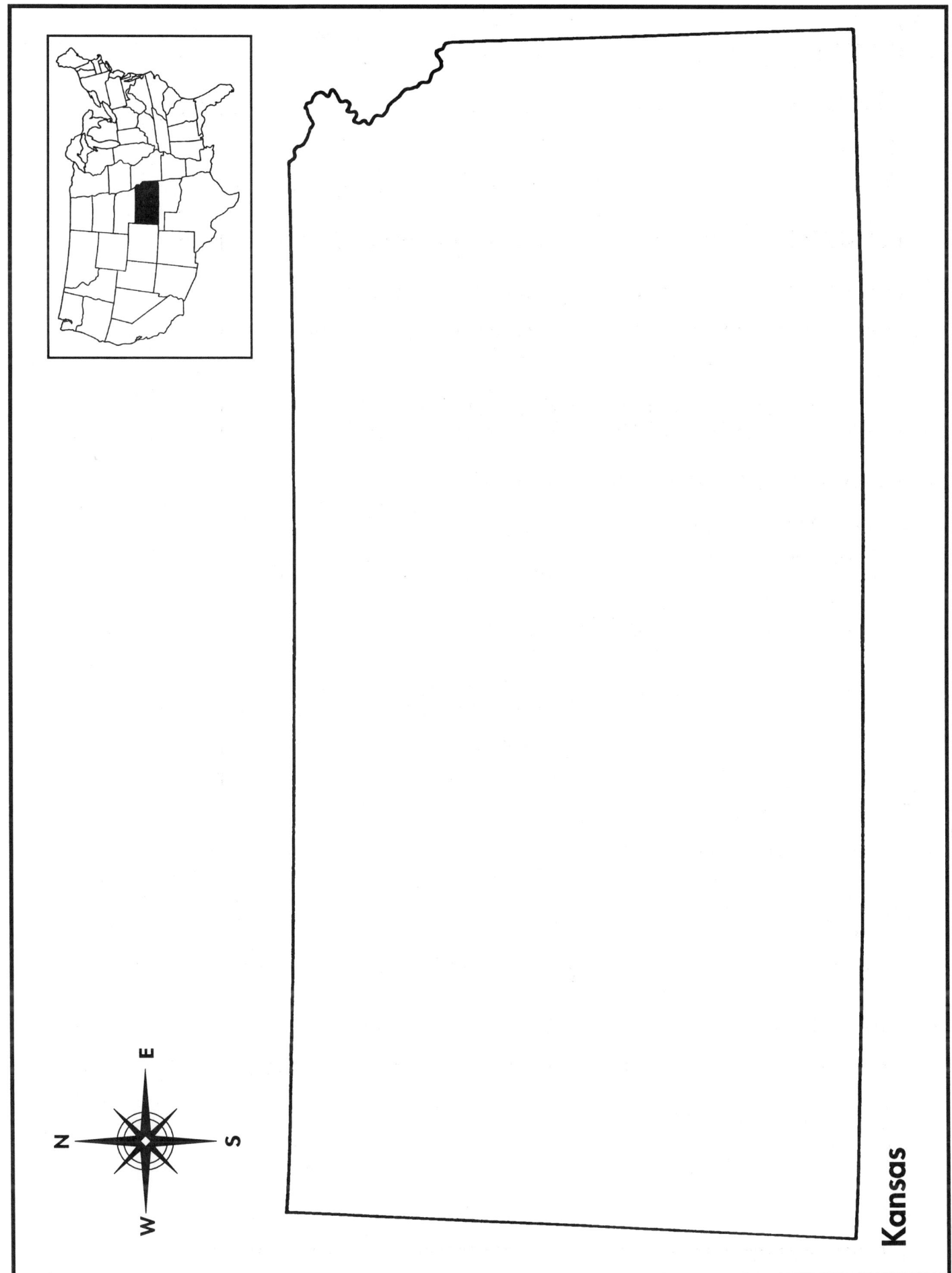

Kansas

U.S. Outline Maps & State Studies: 39

Bluegrass State

Name _____

Date _____

First Non-Native American Settlement:
   James Harrod and colonists from Pennsylvania established Kentucky's first permanent white settlement in 1774. It was built where Harrodsburg is today.

Organized as a Territory: Kentucky was never a territory of the United States.

Admitted to the Union: June 1, 1792 — the 15th state admitted into the Union.

Location: Eastern-Central Region of the United States — part of the Southern States.

State Abbreviations: Ky. (traditional use); KY (post office use).

Capital City: Frankfort became the first permanent capital city in 1793.

Land Area: 39,732 square miles.   Ranks 36th in size among all of the 50 states.
                  (9th in size among the 14 Southern States.)

Population (1995 approximate): 3,850,000 people. Ranks 24th among all states.

   Density: 96 people per square mile.
   Distribution: 52% urban (city).   48% rural (non-city).

Largest City: Louisville — approximate population is 275,000 people.

Highest Elevation: Black Mountain — 4,145 feet above sea level.

State Motto: "United We Stand, Divided We Fall."

Important Historical Events: (a.) Abraham Lincoln was born in a tiny log cabin near Hodgenville. (b.) Although considered a Southern State, Kentucky stayed in the Union and fought against the South and slavery during the Civil War (1861-1865). (c.) Ft. Knox was built in 1936 to house the federal government's gold reserve. It is located about 30 miles south of Louisville.

Kentucky's Animals ❖ Plants ❖ Symbols

Bird: Kentucky Cardinal   **Flower:** Goldenrod   **Tree:** Coffee Tree

Song: *"My Old Kentucky Home"*

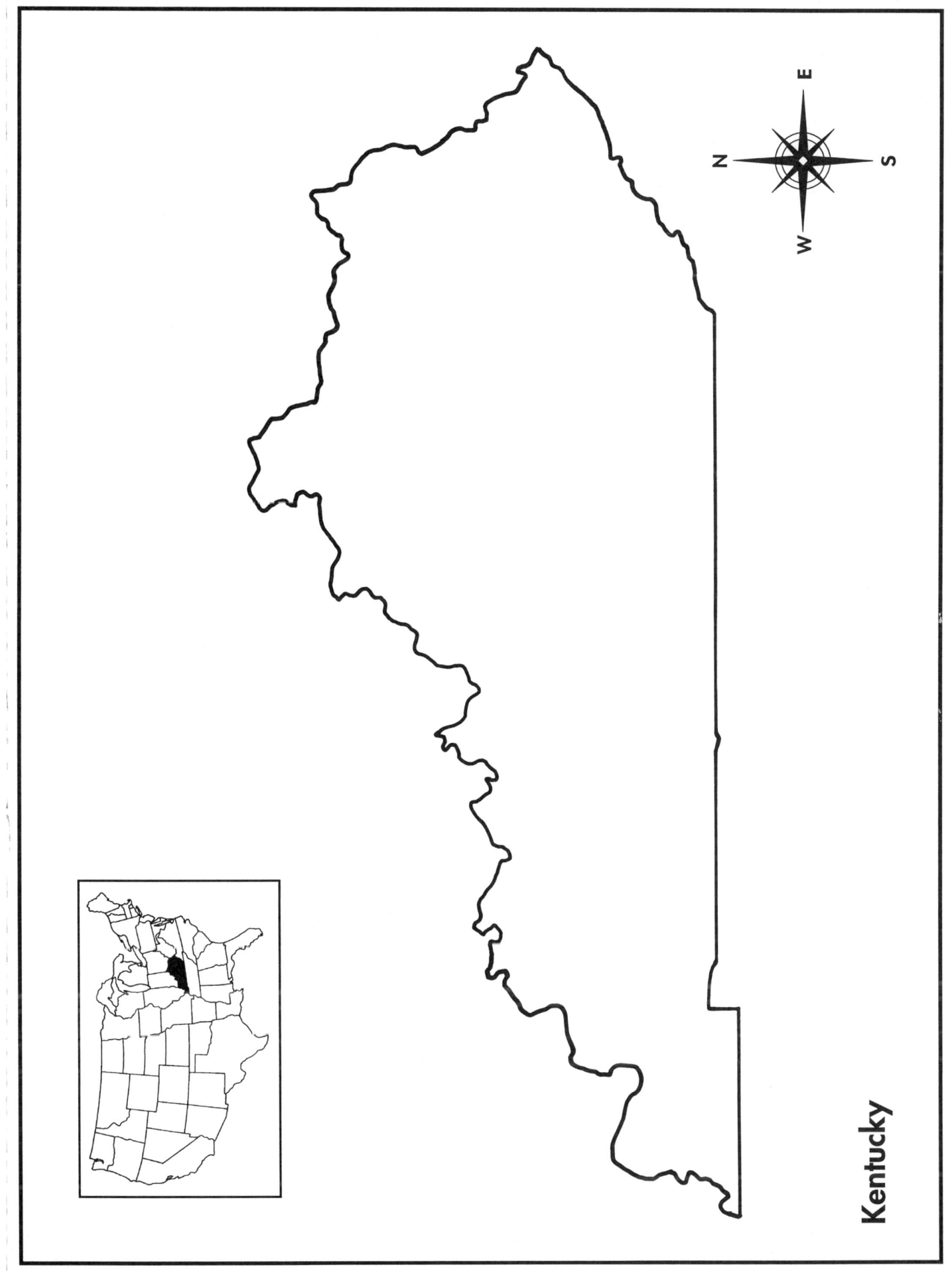

Pelican State ❖ *Creole State* ❖ *Sugar State*

Name _____

Date _____

First Non-Native American Settlement:
A trader named Louis Juchereau de St. Denis established the first permanent settlement on the banks of the Red River. This was in 1714. He named the settlement Natchitoches.

Organized as a Territory: March 26, 1804.

Admitted to the Union: April 30, 1812 — the 18th state admitted into the Union.

Location: South Central Region of the United States — part of the Southern States.

State Abbreviations: La. (traditional use); LA (post office use).

Capital City: Baton Rouge became the capital city in 1882. Other capitals were New Orleans (1812-1830, 1831-1849 and 1862-1882); Donaldsonville (1830-1831); and Baton Rouge (1849-1862).

Land Area: 43,566 square miles. Ranks 33rd in size among all of the 50 states. (7th in size among the 14 Southern States.)

Population (1995 approximate): 4,300,000 people. Ranks 21st among all states.

Density: 99 people per square mile.
Distribution: 66% urban (city).   34% rural (non-city).

Largest City: New Orleans — approximate population is 500,000 people.

Highest Elevation: Driskill Mountain — 535 feet above sea level.

State Motto: "Union, Justice and Confidence."

Important Historical Event: In 1956, the Lake Pontchartrain Causeway opened. This new bridge extended almost 29 miles long, making it the longest in the world.

Louisiana's Animals ❖ Plants ❖ Symbols

Bird: Brown Pelican   **Flower:** Magnolia   **Tree:** Bald Cypress

Song: "Give Me Louisiana"

U.S. Outline Maps & State Studies: 42   © Golden Educational Center

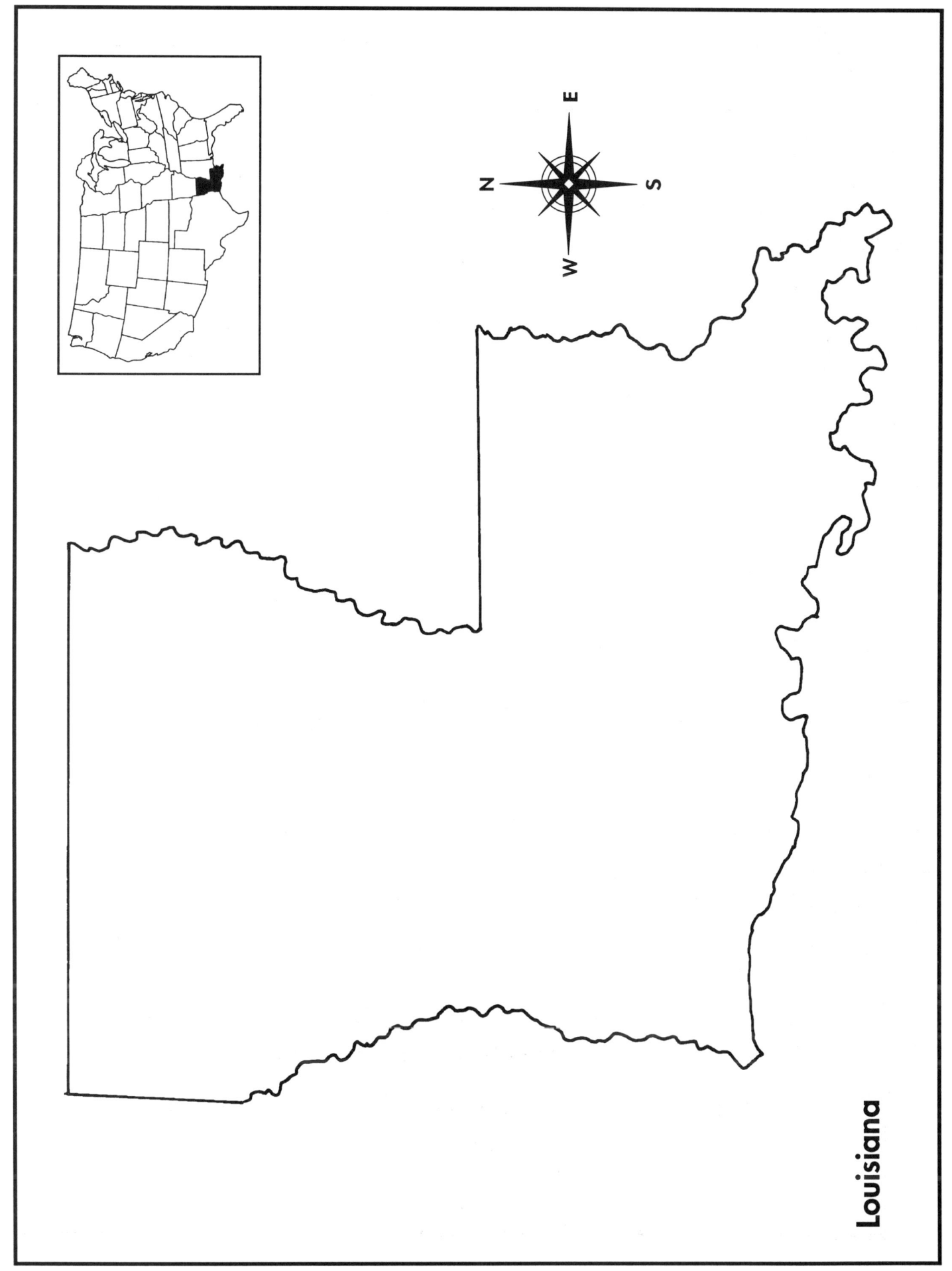

Maine
Pine Tree State

Name _____

Date _____

First Non-Native American Settlement:
The Popham Colony was the state's first permanent settlement in 1607. The English colonists established Popham near the mouth of the Kennebec River.

Organized as a Territory: Maine was never a territory of the United States.

Admitted to the Union: March 15, 1820 — the 23rd state admitted into the Union.

Location: Northeastern Region of the United States — part of the New England States.

State Abbreviations: Me. (traditional use); ME (post office use).

Capital City: Augusta became the capital city in 1832. Portland was the capital from 1820 to 1832.

Land Area: 30,865 square miles. Ranks 39th in size among all of the 50 states. (1st in size among the 6 New England States.)

Population (1995 approximate)**:** 1,350,000 people. Ranks 39th among all states.

Density: 40 people per square mile.
Distribution: 51% urban (city).   49% rural (non-city).

Largest City: Portland — approximate population is 65,000 people.

Highest Elevation: Mt. Katahdin — 5,268 feet above sea level.

State Motto: *"Dirigo."* (I Direct; or I Guide.)

Important Historical Event: In 1775, the first naval battle of the Revolutionary War was fought off of Machias. The "Patriots" captured the British armed schooner named *Margaretta*.

Maine's Animals ❖ Plants ❖ Symbols

Bird: Chickadee   **Tree:** White Pine

Mineral: Tourmaline   **Fish:** Landlocked Salmon

Flower: White Pine Cone & Tassel

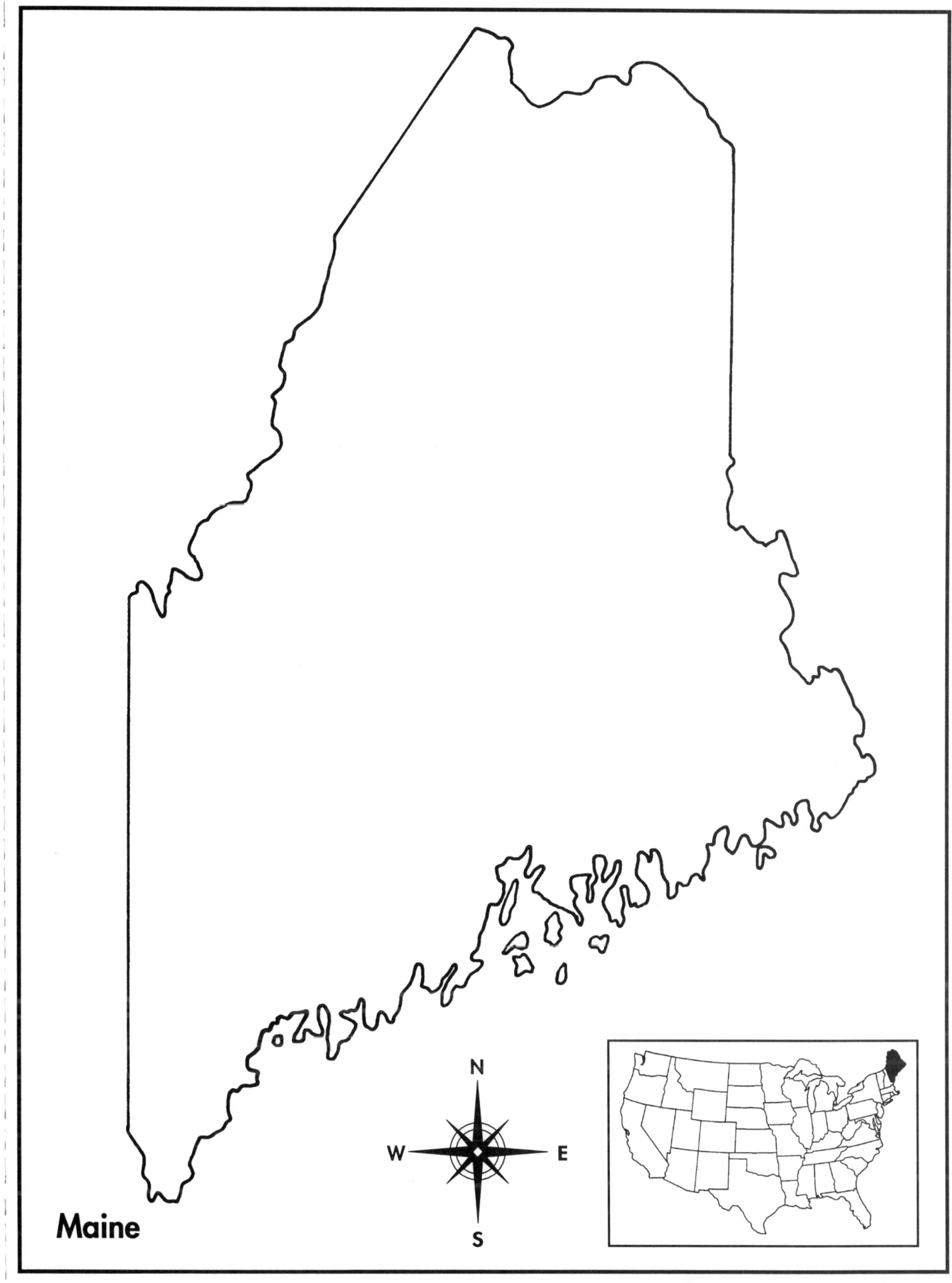

Old Line State ❖ *Free State*

Name _____

Date _____

First Non-Native American Settlement:
    The first settlement of white men was on Kent Island. William Claiborne, a Virginia planter, established a trading post there in 1631. A year later, an Englishman named Leonard Calvert landed on Saint Clements Island and founded the colony of Maryland.

Organized as a Territory: Maryland was never a territory of the United States.

Admitted to the Union: April 28, 1788 — the 7th state admitted into the Union.

Location: Eastern-Central Region of the United States — part of the Southern States.

State Abbreviations: Md. (traditional use); MD (post office use).

Capital City: Annapolis became the capital city in 1694. St. Mary's was the capital from 1634 until 1694.

Land Area: 9,775 square miles.   Ranks 42nd in size among all of the 50 states. (13th in size among the 14 Southern States.)

Population (1995 approximate): 4,925,000 people. Ranks 19th among all states.

    Density: 504 people per square mile.
    Distribution: 77% urban (city).   23% rural (non-city).

Largest City: Baltimore — approximate population is 750,000 people.

Highest Elevation: Backbone Mountain — 3,360 feet above sea level.

State Motto: "Fatti Maschii, Parole Femine." (Manly Deeds, Womanly Words)

Important Historical Events: (a.) In 1791, Maryland gave land to the Federal government for the District of Columbia (Washington, D.C.). (b.) In 1864, a state constitution was adopted that abolished slavery in Maryland.

Maryland's Animals ❖ Plants ❖ Symbols

Bird: Baltimore Oriole   **Flower:** Black-eyed Susan
Crustacean: Md. Blue Crab   **Dog:** Chesapeake Bay Retriever
Tree: White Oak   **Boat:** Skipjack   **Sport:** Jousting
Fish: Rockfish   **Insect:** Baltimore Checkerspot Butterfly

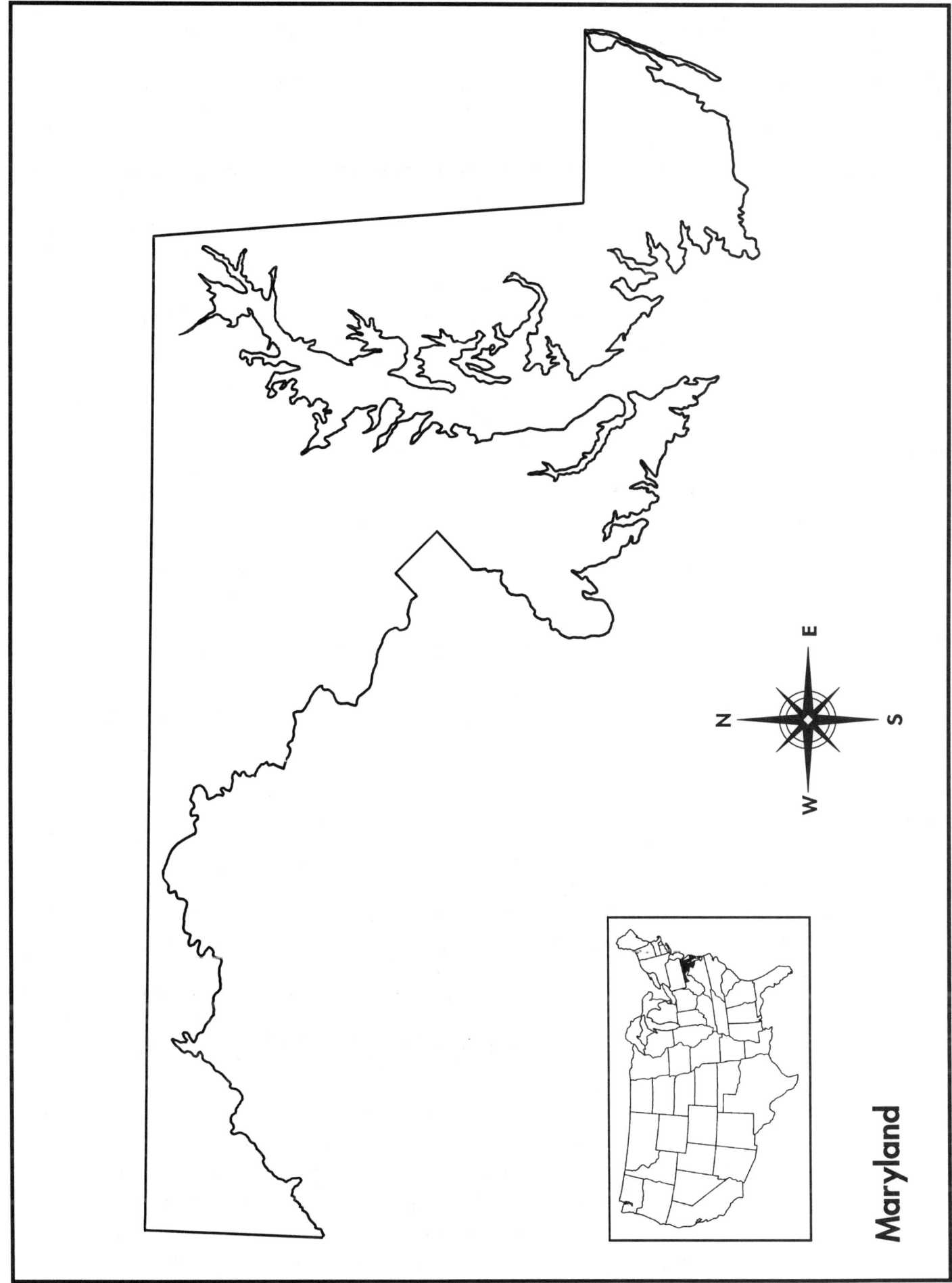

Maryland

© GOLDEN EDUCATIONAL CENTER

U.S. Outline Maps & State Studies: 47

Massachusetts

Bay State ❖ *Old Colony State*

Name _____

Date _____

First Non-Native American Settlement:

    On September 16, 1620, a group of Pilgrims set sail on the *Mayflower* from Plymouth, England. That November, the Pilgrims landed in what is now Provincetown Harbor. A month later they sailed across Cape Cod Bay and established the settlement of Plymouth.

Organized as a Territory: Massachusetts was never a territory of the United States.

Admitted to the Union: February 6, 1788 — the 6th state admitted into the Union.

Location: Northeastern Region of the United States — part of the New England States.

State Abbreviations: Mass. (traditional use); MA (post office use).

Capital City: Boston became the capital city in 1630. It is the only capital the state has had.

Land Area: 7,838 square miles.   Ranks 45th in size among all of the 50 states.
        (4th in size among the 6 New England States.)

Population (1995 approximate): 6,000,000 people. Ranks 13th among all states.

    Density: 766 people per square mile.
    Distribution: 85% urban (city).   15% rural (non-city).

Largest City: Boston — approximate population is 580,000 people.

Highest Elevation: Mt. Greylock — 3,491 feet above sea level.

State Motto: "By the sword we seek peace, but peace only under liberty."

Important Historical Events: (a.) In 1636, Harvard became the first college in the colonies. (b.) The Boston Tea Party of December 16, 1773, led to the start of the Revolutionary War. (c.) Stephen Daye set up the colony's first printing press at Cambridge in 1639.

Massachusetts' Animals ❖ Plants ❖ Symbols

Bird: Chickadee   **Flower:** Mayflower   **Tree:** American Elm

Colors: Blue & Gold   **Insect:** Ladybug

Beverage: Cranberry Juice   **Muffin:** Corn Muffin

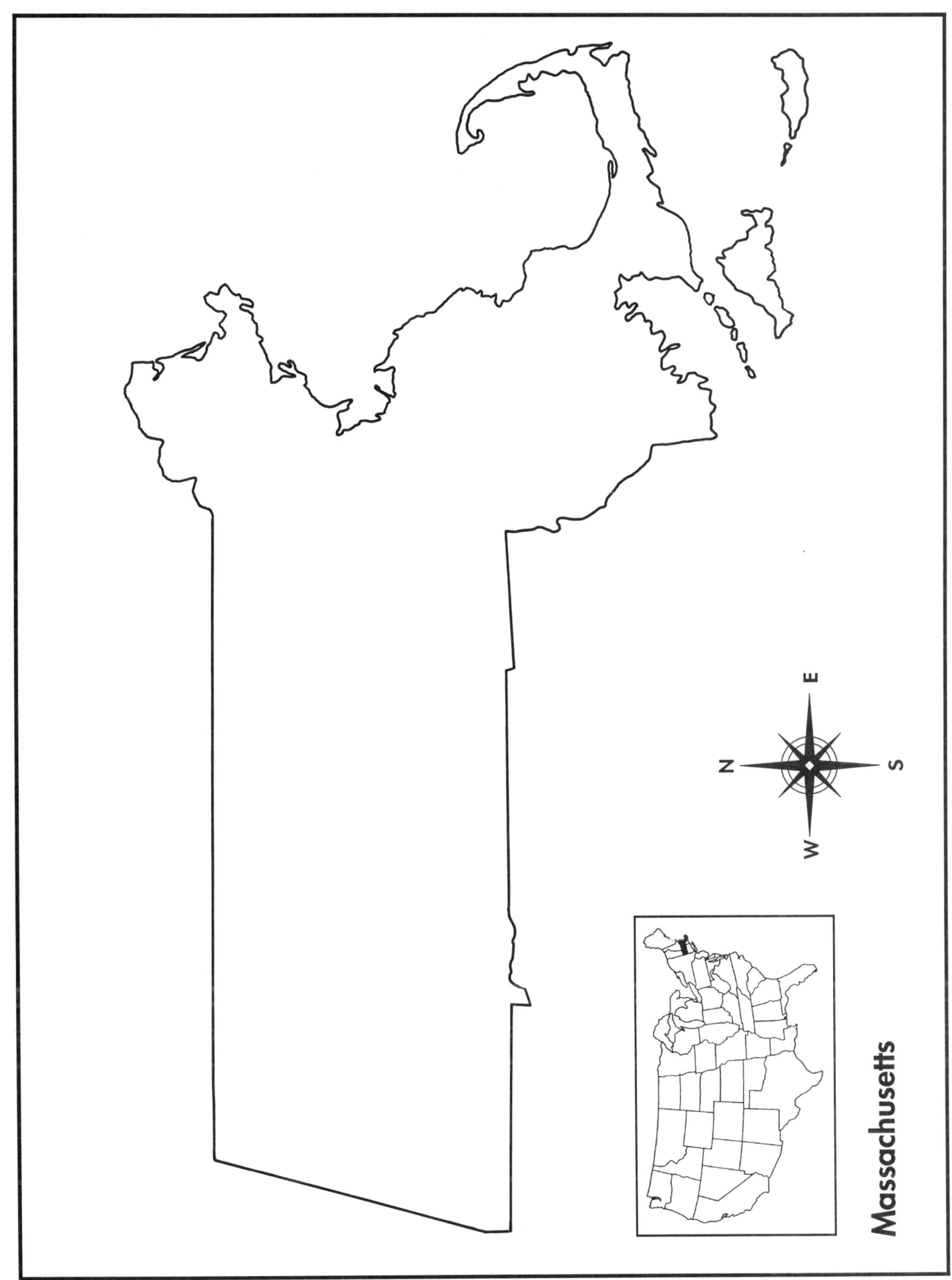

The Wolverine State

Name _____

Date _____

First Non-Native American Settlement:
In 1668, Father Marquette founded Michigan's first permanent settlement at Sault Sainte Marie.

Organized as a Territory: January 11, 1805.

Admitted to the Union: January 26, 1837 — the 26th state admitted into the Union.

Location: North-Central Region of the United States — part of the Midwestern States.

State Abbreviations: Mich. (traditional use); MI (post office use).

Capital City: Lansing has been the capital city since 1847. Detroit was the capital from 1837-1847.

Land Area: 58,110 square miles.   Ranks 22nd in size among all of the 50 states. (7th in size among the 12 Midwestern States.)

Population (1995 approximate): 9,500,000 people. Ranks 8th among all states.

Density: 164 people per square mile.
Distribution: 74% urban (city). 26% rural (non-city).

Largest City: Detroit — approximate population is 1,050,000 people.

Highest Elevation: Mt. Curwood — 1,980 feet above sea level.

State Motto: "If you seek a pleasant peninsula, look around you."

Important Historical Events: (a.) Detroit, the 6th largest city in the nation, was founded at St. Pontchartrain in 1701, by the French explorer Cadillac. (b.) In 1861, Thomas Edison built his first electric battery at Ft. Gratiot (Port Huron). (c.) Henry Ford built his first workable automobile in Detroit in 1896. Three years later, Ransom Olds built Michigan's first automobile factory at Detroit.

Michigan's Animals ❖ Plants ❖ Symbols

Bird: Robin   **Flower:** Apple Blossom   **Tree:** White Pine

Flag: Blue charged with the arms of the state   **Fishes:** Trout & Brook Trout

Gem: Isle Royal Greenstone (Chlorastrolite)   **Soil:** Kalkaska Soil Series

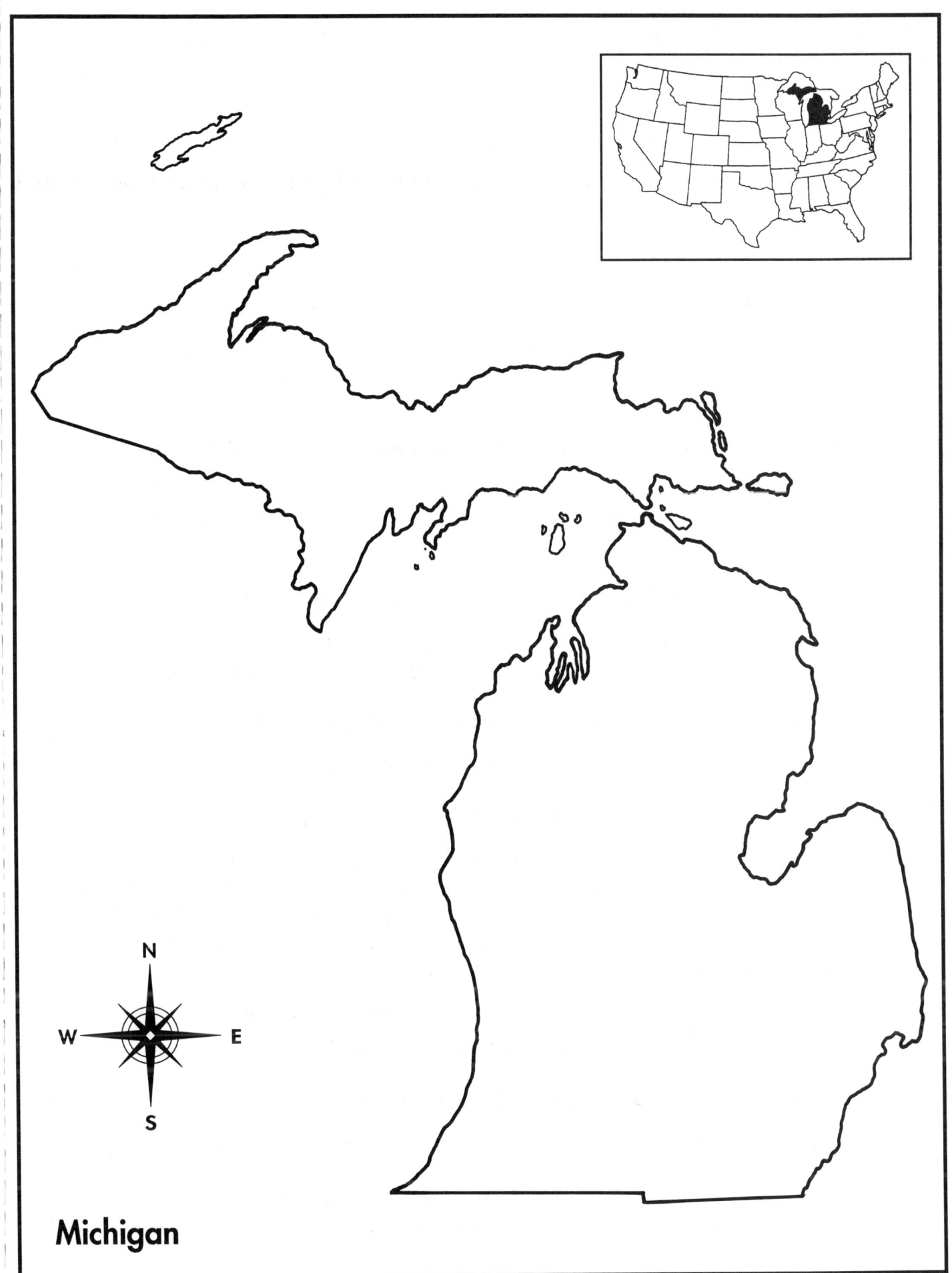

Minnesota

Gopher State ❖ North Star State

Name _____

Date _____

First Non-Native American Settlement:
From 1820-1822, American soldiers built Fort St. Anthony (renamed Fort Snelling in 1825). The fort was built where the Minnesota and Mississippi Rivers meet in the southeastern part of the state.

Organized as a Territory: March 3, 1849.

Admitted to the Union: May 11, 1858 — the 32nd state admitted into the Union.

Location: North-Central Region of the United States — part of the Midwestern States.

State Abbreviations: Minn. (traditional use); MN (post office use).

Capital City: St. Paul has been the capital city since 1849. It has been the state's only capital.

Land Area: 79,617 square miles.   Ranks 14th in size among all of the 50 states.
(2nd in size among the 12 Midwestern States.)

Population (1995 approximate): 4,500,000 people. Ranks 20th among all states.

Density: 57 people per square mile.
Distribution: 66% urban (city). 34% rural (non-city).

Largest City: Minneapolis — approximate population is 375,000 people.

Highest Elevation: Eagle Mountain — 2,301 feet above sea level.

State Motto: "L'Etoile du Nord." (The North Star.)

Important Historical Events: (a.) In 1803, the United States obtained the western part of the Minnesota area through the Louisiana Purchase. (b.) Henry Schoolcraft discovered the source of the Mississippi River at Lake Itasca. (c.) The Mayo Clinic is one of the greatest medical research centers in the world. It was established at Rochester in 1889 by William W. Mayo and his two sons.

Minnesota's Animals ❖ Plants ❖ Symbols

Flower: Showy Lady Slipper   **Tree:** Red (or Norway) Pine

Mushroom: Morel   **Fish:** Walleye

Bird: Common Loon (also called Great Northern Diver)

U.S. Outline Maps & State Studies: 52   © Golden Educational Center

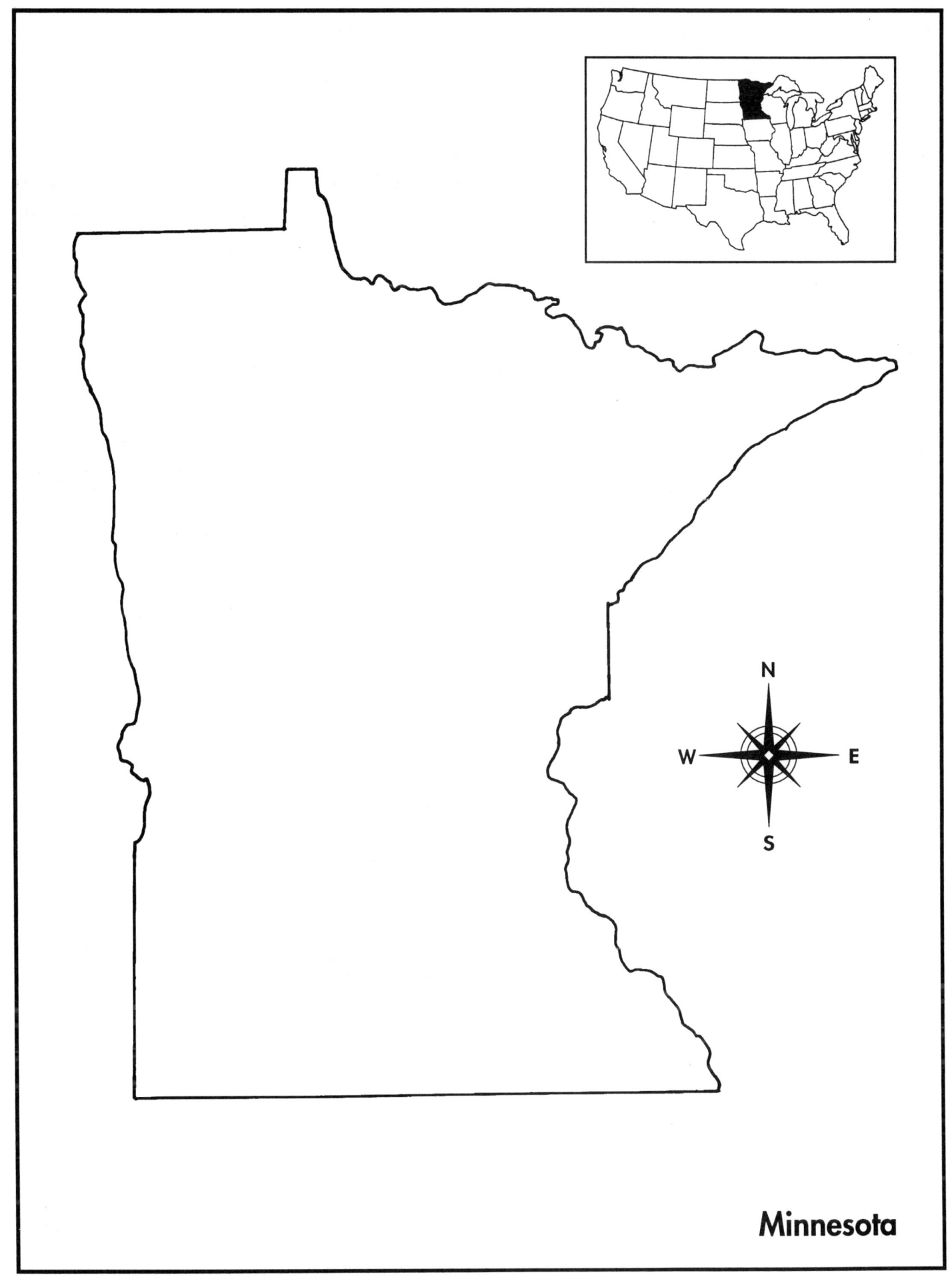

Mississippi
Magnolia State

Name _____

Date _____

First Non-Native American Settlement:
   In 1699, a French explorer, established the first settlement of the region at Old Biloxi (now Ocean Springs). In 1719, the first African slaves were brought to the region from West Africa. It took almost 150 years, one war and many lives to abolish slavery in the United States.

Organized as a Territory: April 7, 1798.

Admitted to the Union: December 10, 1817 — the 20th state admitted into the Union.

Location: South-Central Region of the United States — part of the Southern States.

State Abbreviations: Miss. (traditional use); MS (post office use).

Capital City: Jackson has been the capital city since 1822. Earlier capitals were Natchez (1798-1802 and 1817-1821), Washington (1802-1817) and Columbia (1821-1822).

Land Area: 46,914 square miles.   Ranks 31st in size among all of the 50 states.
(6th in size among the 14 Southern States.)

Population (1995 approximate): 2,625,000 people. Ranks 31st among all states.

   Density: 56 people per square mile.
   Distribution: 45% urban (city).   55% rural (non-city).

Largest City: Jackson — approximate population is 200,000 people.

Highest Elevation: Woodall Mountain — 806 feet above sea level.

State Motto: "Virtute Et Armis." (By Valor and Arms.)

Important Historical Event: In 1964, atomic scientists set off the first nuclear bomb test east of the Mississippi River. They set the explosion off at Baxterville, Mississippi.

Mississippi's Animals ❖ Plants ❖ Symbols

Bird: Mockingbird   **Flower:** Magnolia Blossom   **Tree:** Magnolia
Stone: Petrified Wood   **Fish:** Large-mouth or Black Bass
Insect: Honeybee   **Land Mammal:** White-tailed Deer   **Beverage:** Milk
Water Mammal: Bottlenosed Dolphin or Porpoise

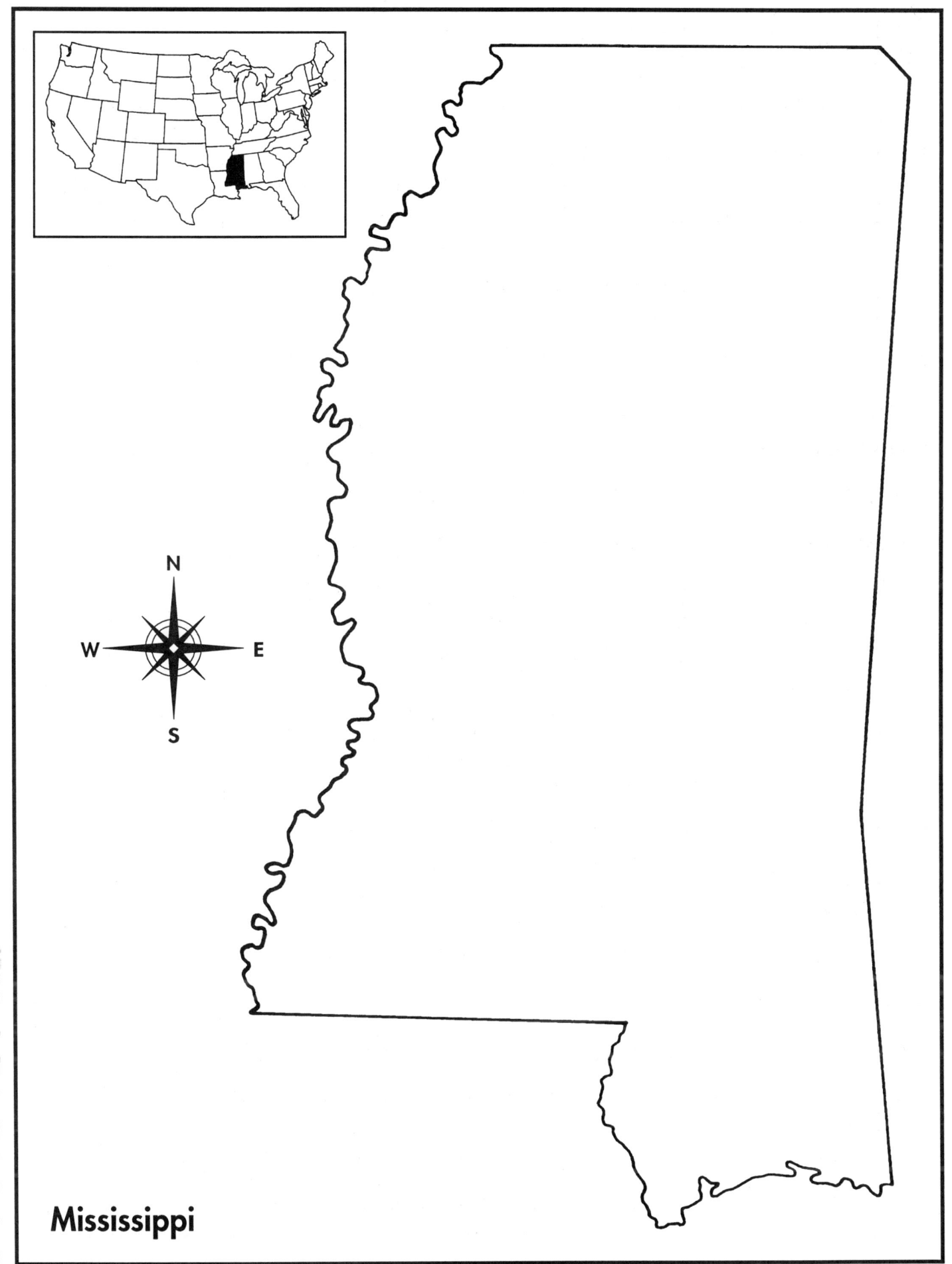

 Missouri

Show-Me State

First Non-Native American Settlement:
French settlers came from what is today's Illinois and established Missouri's first permanent settlement. The settlement was named Sainte Genevieve. It was established in 1735.

Organized as a Territory: June 4, 1812.

Admitted to the Union: August 10, 1821 — the 24th state admitted into the Union.

Location: Central Region of the United States — part of the Midwestern States.

State Abbreviations: Mo. (traditional use); MO (post office use).

Capital City: Jefferson City has been the capital city since 1826. The other capital cities were St. Louis (1820) and St. Charles (1821-1826).

Land Area: 68,898 square miles. Ranks 18th in size among all of the 50 states. (6th in size among the 12 Midwestern States.)

Population (1995 approximate): 5,250,000 people. Ranks 16th among all states.

Density: 75 people per square mile.
Distribution: 70% urban (city). 30% rural (non-city).

Largest City: Kansas City — approximate population is 450,000 people.

Highest Elevation: Taum Sauk Mountain — 1,772 feet above sea level.

State Motto: "The welfare of the people shall be the supreme law."

Important Historical Events: (a.) Lewis and Clark began their famous journey from near St. Louis in 1804. (b.) "The Missouri Compromise," passed by Congress in 1820, brought Missouri into the Union as a slave state.

Missouri's Animals ❖ Plants ❖ Symbols

Bird: Bluebird	**Flower:** Hawthorn	**Insect:** Honeybee
Tree Nut: Black Walnut	**Tree:** Flowering Dogwood	**Rock:** Mozarkite
Musical Instrument: Fiddle	**Mineral:** Galena	**Fossil:** Crinoidea

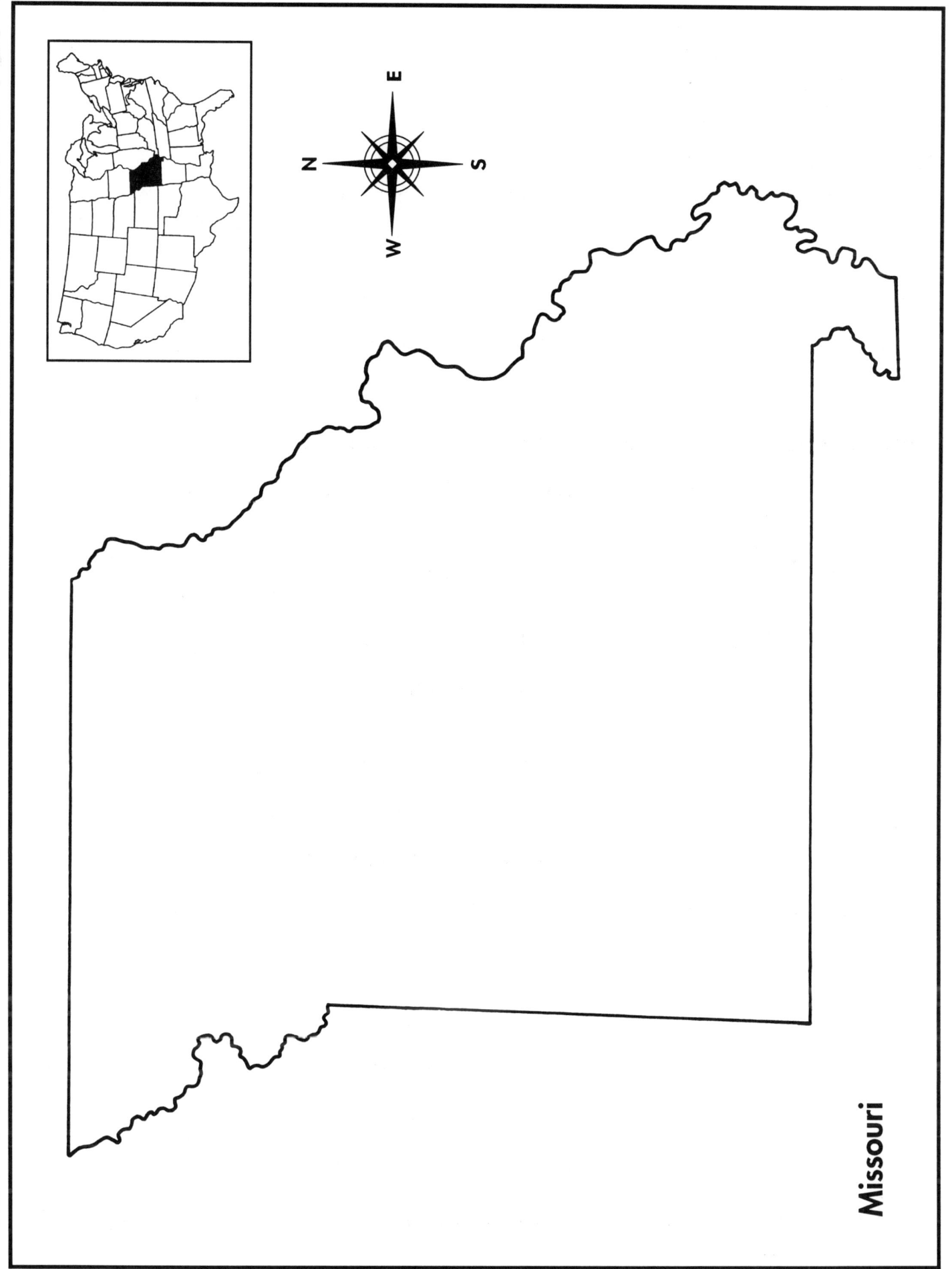

Missouri

U.S. Outline Maps & State Studies: 57

Montana

The Treasure State

Name _____

Date _____

First Non-Native American Settlement:
In 1847, the American Fur Company built the first permanent settlement in Montana at Fort Benton on the Missouri River. The United States received most of the territory as part of the Louisiana Purchase in 1803.

Organized as a Territory: May 26, 1864.

Admitted to the Union: November 8, 1889 — the 41st state admitted into the Union.

Location: Northwestern Region of the U.S. — part of the Rocky Mountain States.

State Abbreviations: Mont. (traditional use); MT (post office use).

Capital City: Helena became the capital city in 1875. The other capitals were Bannock (1864-1865) and Virginia City (1865-1875).

Land Area: 145,556 square miles. Ranks 4th in size among all of the 50 states. (1st in size among the 6 Rocky Mountain States.)

Population (1995 approximate): 850,000 people. Ranks 44th among all states.

Density: 6 people per square mile.
Distribution: 53% urban (city).   47% rural (non-city).

Largest City: Billings — approximate population is 85,000 people.

Highest Elevation: Granite Peak — 12,799 feet above sea level.

State Motto: *"Oro y Plata."* (Gold and Silver.)

Important Historical Event: In 1880, the Utah & Northern Railroad began laying track in Montana. Two years later, the Northern Pacific Railroad (renamed) crossed the state.

Montana's Animals ❖ Plants ❖ Symbols

Bird: Western Meadowlark

Tree: Ponderosa Pine

Stones: Sapphire & Agate

Flower: Bitterroot

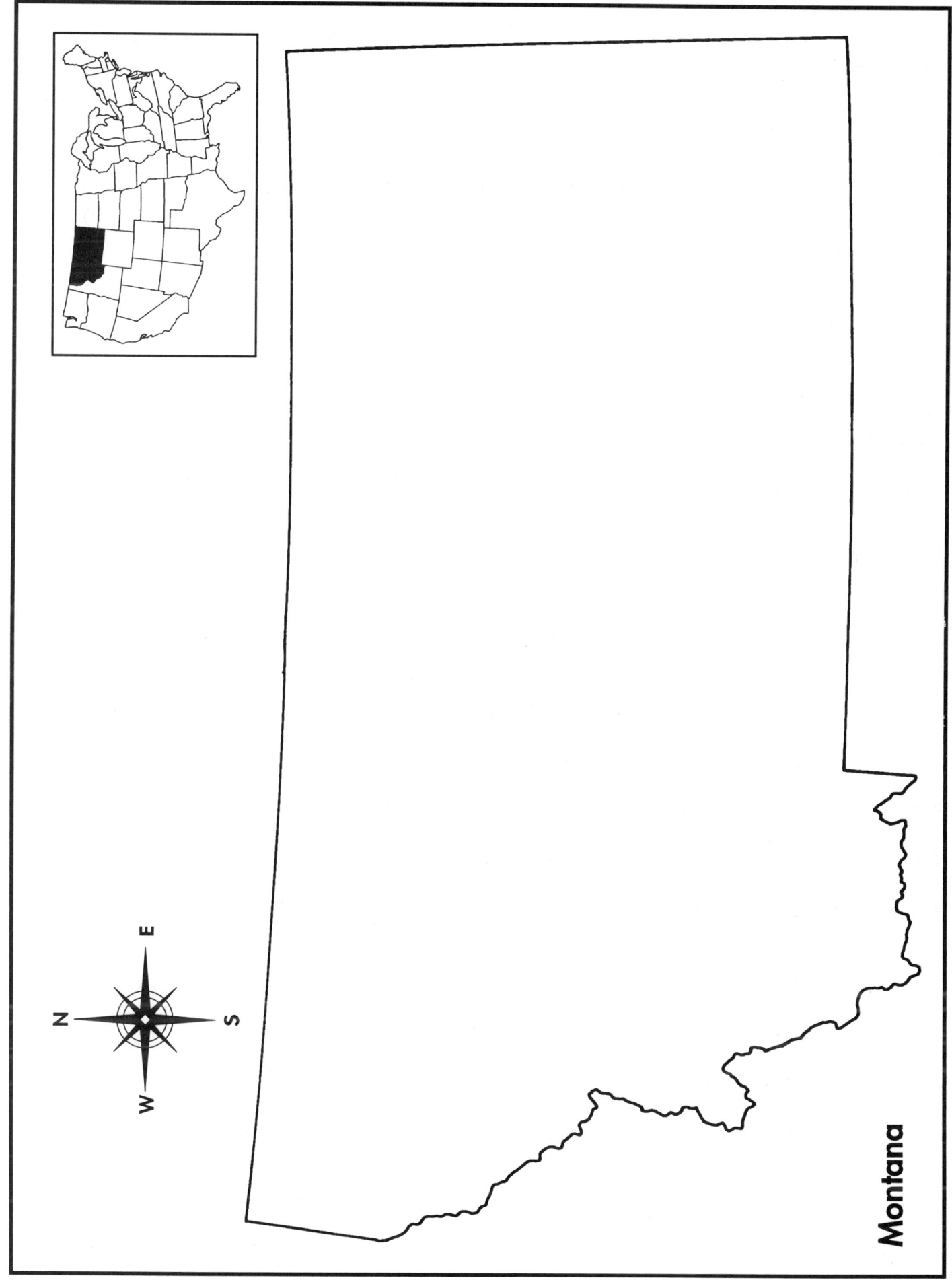

Montana

Nebraska

Cornhusker State (1945) ❖ *Beef State*
Tree Planter State (1895)

Name _____

Date _____

First Non-Native American Settlement:
　　Bellevue was the first permanent settlement in Nebraska. It was founded in 1823. The U.S. Army built Fort Atkinson in 1819, about 16 miles north of today's Omaha. The fort had Nebraska's first school, library, sawmill and brickyard. It was abandoned in 1827.

Organized as a Territory: May 30, 1854.

Admitted to the Union: March 1, 1867 — the 37th state admitted into the Union.

Location: Central Region of the United States — part of the Midwestern States.

State Abbreviations: Nebr. (traditional use); NE (post office use).

Capital City: Lincoln has been the capital since 1867. Omaha was the capital from 1855 to 1867.

Land Area: 76,878 square miles.　　Ranks 15th in size among all of the 50 states. (3rd in size among the 12 Midwestern States.)

Population (1995 approximate): 1,625,000 people. Ranks 36th among all states.

　　　　Density: 21 people per square mile.
　　　　Distribution: 62% urban (city).　　38% rural (non-city).

Largest City: Omaha — approximate population is 350,000 people.

Highest Elevation: Southwestern Kimball County — 5,426 feet above sea level.

State Motto: "Equality before the law."

Important Historical Event: Nebraska's one-house legislature was adopted in 1934. This is the only state government of its kind in the entire United States. (The other states have two-house legislatures — one is the Senate and the other is the House of Representatives.)

Nebraska's Animals ❖ Plants ❖ Symbols

Bird: Western Meadowlark　　**Flower:** Goldenrod　　**Tree:** Cottonwood

Insect: Honeybee　　**Mammal:** White-tailed Deer　　**Rock:** Prairie Agate

Gemstone: Blue Agate　　　　　　　　　　　　**Fossil:** Mammoth

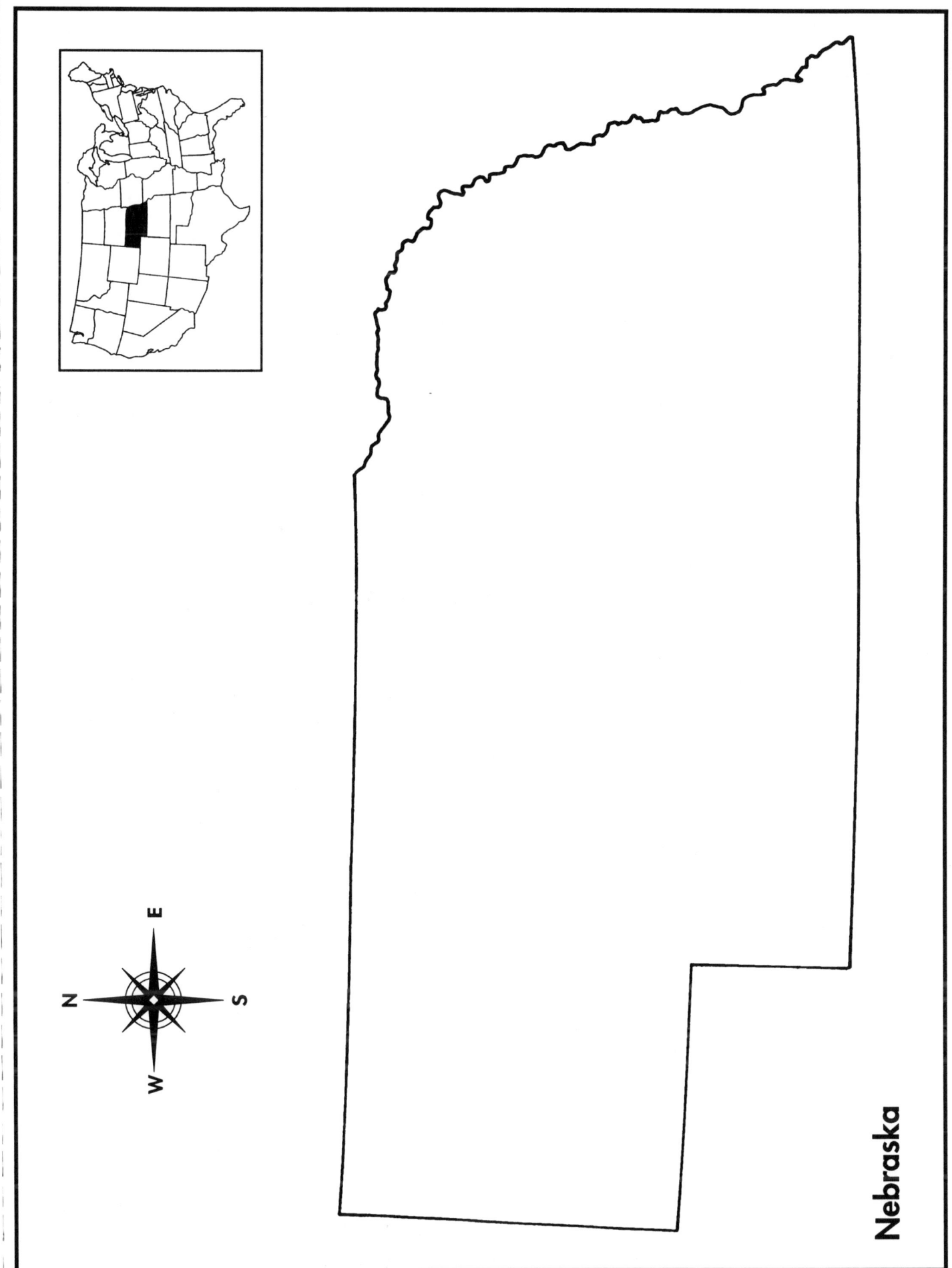

 Nevada

Name _____

Date _____

Sagebrush State ❖ Silver State
Battle-born State

First Non-Native American Settlement:
    Mormons from Utah's Great Salt Lake area built a trading station at Mormon Station (present-day Genoa) in the Carson Valley. The post provided supplies for gold seekers on their way to California.

Organized as a Territory: March 2, 1861.

Admitted to the Union: October 31, 1864 — the 36th state admitted into the Union.

Location: Western-Central Region of the U.S. — part of the Rocky Mountain States.

State Abbreviations: Nev. (traditional use); NV (post office use).

Capital City: Carson City has been the capital since the Nevada Territory was created in 1861.

Land Area: 109,806 square miles.   Ranks 7th in size among all of the 50 states.
        (2nd in size among the 6 Rocky Mountain States.)

Population (1995 approximate): 1,425,000 people. Ranks 38th among all states.

    Density: 13 people per square mile.
    Distribution: 85% urban (city).   15% rural (non-city).

Largest City: Las Vegas — approximate population is 270,000 people.

Highest Elevation: Boundary Peak — 13,143 feet above sea level.

State Motto: "All for our country."

Important Historical Event: Hoover Dam (named after President Herbert Hoover) was completed in 1936. Its reservoir, Lake Mead, is one of the largest man-made lakes in the world. It is 115 miles long.

Nevada's Animals ❖ Plants ❖ Symbols

Bird: Mountain Bluebird   **Flower:** Sagebrush   **Fish:** Cutthroat Trout
Colors: Silver & Blue   **Animal:** Desert Bighorn Sheep   **Reptile:** Tortoise
Gemstones: Virgin Valley Black Opal & Nev. Turquoise   **Fossil:** Ichthyosaur
Tree: Single-leaf Pinon & Bristlecone Pine   **Rock:** Sandstone

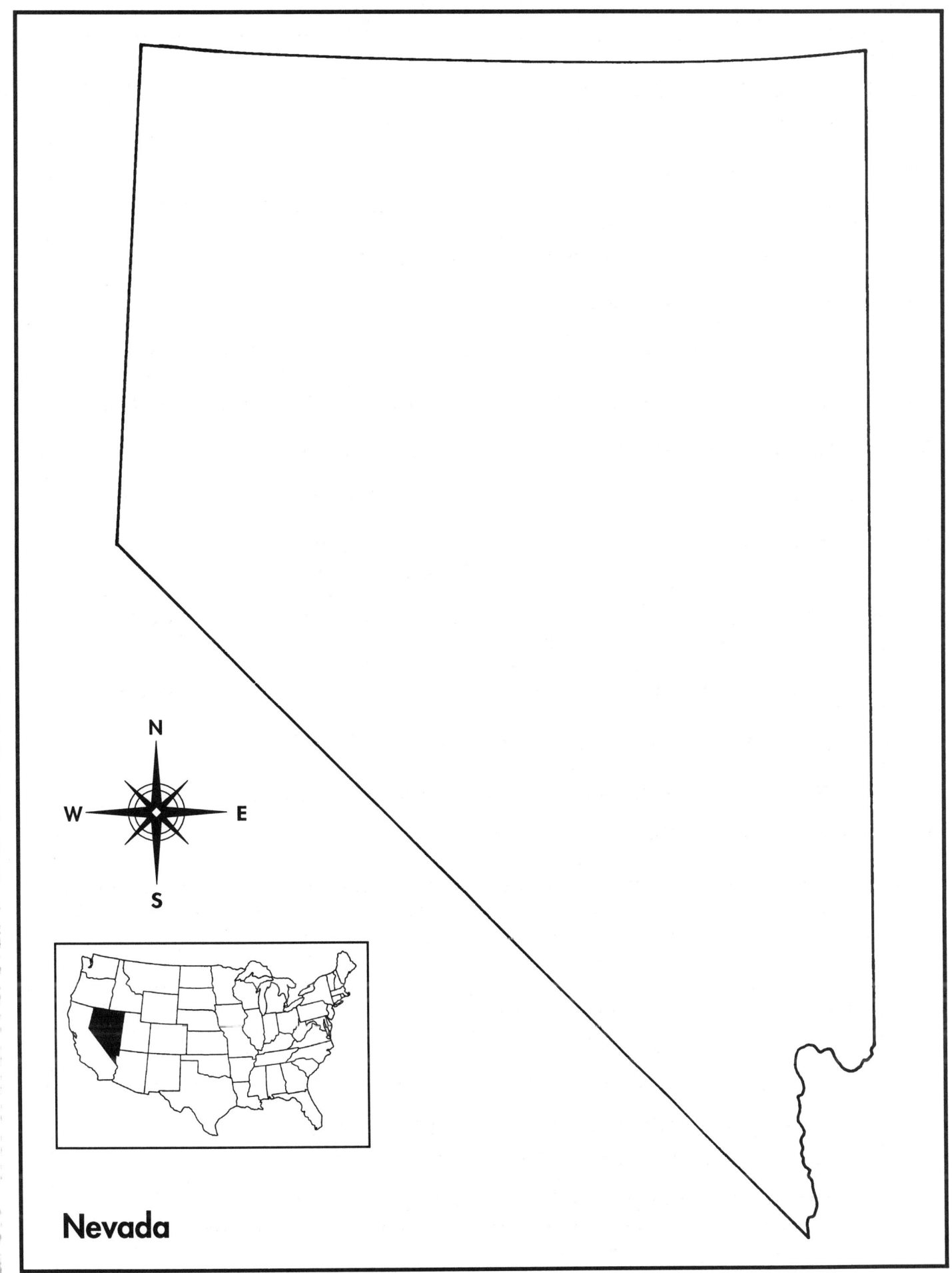

Nevada

New Hampshire

Granite State

Name _____

Date _____

First Non-Native American Settlement:
    In 1623, Englishman David Thompson and a group of settlers, founded the first white settlement in New Hampshire at Odiorne's Point (now part of Rye).

Organized as a Territory: New Hampshire was never a territory of the United States.

Admitted to the Union: June 21, 1788 — the 9th state admitted into the Union.

Location: Northeastern Region of the United States — part of the New England States.

State Abbreviations: N.H. (traditional use); NH (post office use).

Capital City: Concord became the capital city in 1808. Other capitals were Portsmouth (1679-1774), Exeter (1775-1781) and Concord (1782-1784).

Land Area: 8,969 square miles.   Ranks 44th in size among all of the 50 states. (3rd in size among the 6 New England States.)

Population (1995 approximate)**:** 1,125,000 people. Ranks 41st among all states.

    Density: 125 people per square mile.
    Distribution: 56% urban (city).   44% rural (non-city).

Largest City: Manchester — approximate population is 100,000 people.

Highest Elevation: Mt. Washington — 6,288 feet above sea level.

State Motto: "Live free or die."

Important Historical Events: (a.) New Hampshire was the first colony to gain its independence from Britain. The state adopted a constitution on January 6, 1776, six months before the "Declaration of Independence" was signed by the 13 colonies. (b.) In 1961, Alan B. Shepard, Jr. of East Derry, New Hampshire, became the first American to travel in space.

New Hampshire's Animals ❖ Plants ❖ Symbols

Bird: Purple Finch   **Flower:** Purple Lilac   **Tree:** White Birch

---

U.S. Outline Maps & State Studies: 64   © Golden Educational Center

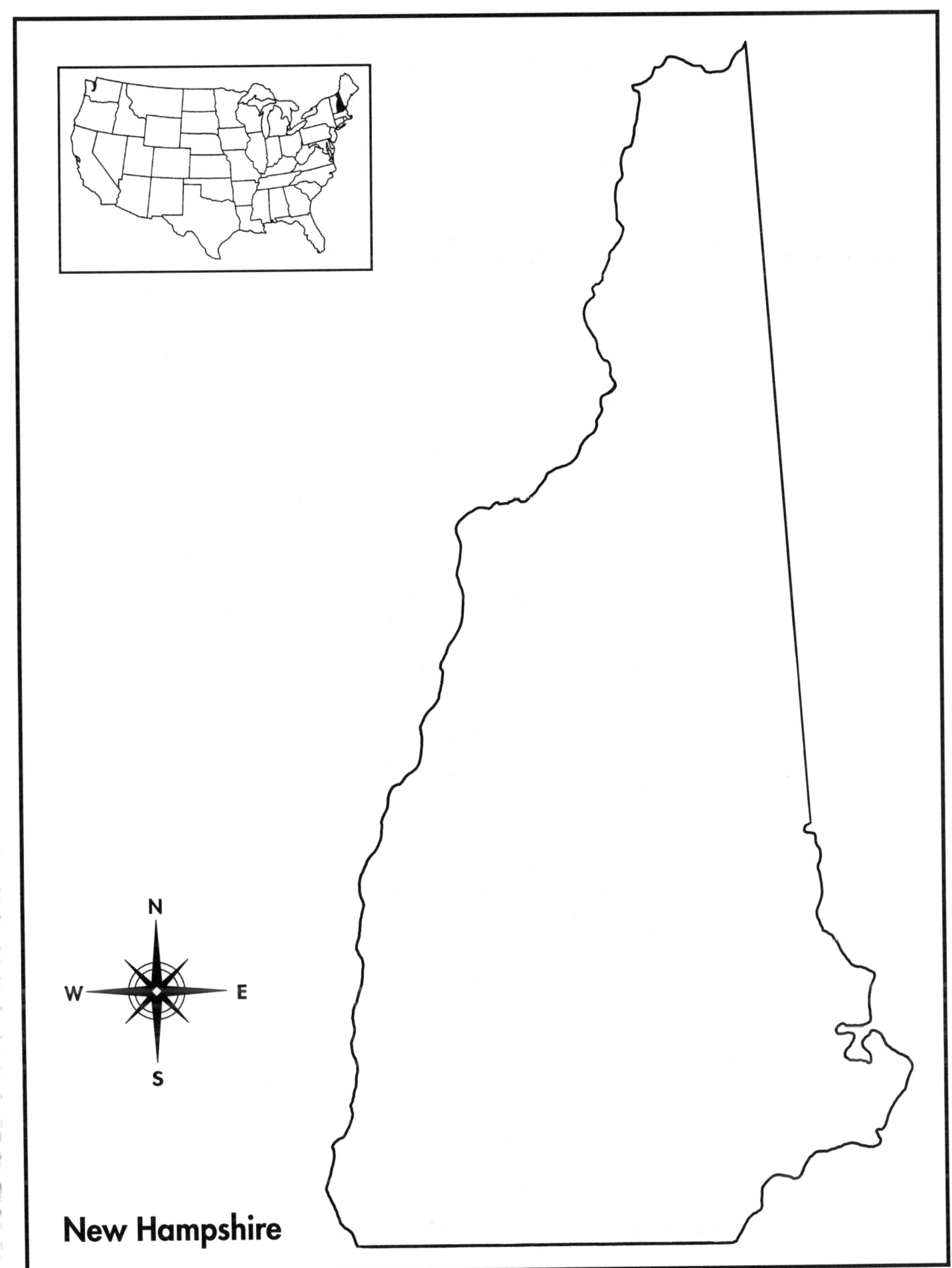

New Jersey
Garden State

Name _____

Date _____

First Non-Native American Settlement:
 The Dutch founded an outpost in Pavonia, which is part of Jersey City, in about 1630. However, a permanent settlement was not possible until 1660.

Organized as a Territory: New Jersey was never a territory of the United States.

Admitted to the Union: December 18, 1787 — the 3rd state admitted into the Union.

Location: Northeastern Coast Region of the U.S. — part of the Middle Atlantic States.

State Abbreviations: N.J. (traditional use); NJ (post office use).

Capital City: Trenton became the capital in 1790. Perth Amboy and Burlington both served as capitals from 1703 to 1775. There was no official capital from 1775 to 1790.

Land Area: 7,419 square miles.   Ranks 46th in size among all of the 50 states. (3rd in size among the 3 Middle Atlantic States.)

Population (1995 approximate)**:** 8,300,000 people. Ranks 9th among all states.

  Density: 1,119 people per square mile.
  Distribution: 89% urban (city).   11% rural (non-city).

Largest City: Newark — approximate population is 300,000 people.

Highest Elevation: High Point (how appropriate the name!) — 1,803 feet above sea level.

State Motto: "Liberty and Prosperity."

Important Historical Events: (a.) From June 30 to November 4, 1783, Princeton University served as the nation's capital. (b.) In 1846, the *New York Nine* defeated the *New York Knickerbockers* in the world's first professional baseball game. (Yes, they were New York teams, playing in New Jersey.)

New Jersey's Animals ❖ Plants ❖ Symbols

Flower: Purple Violet   **Tree:** Red Oak

Colors: Buff & Blue   **Animal:** Horse   **Insect:** Honeybee

Bird: Eastern Goldfinch

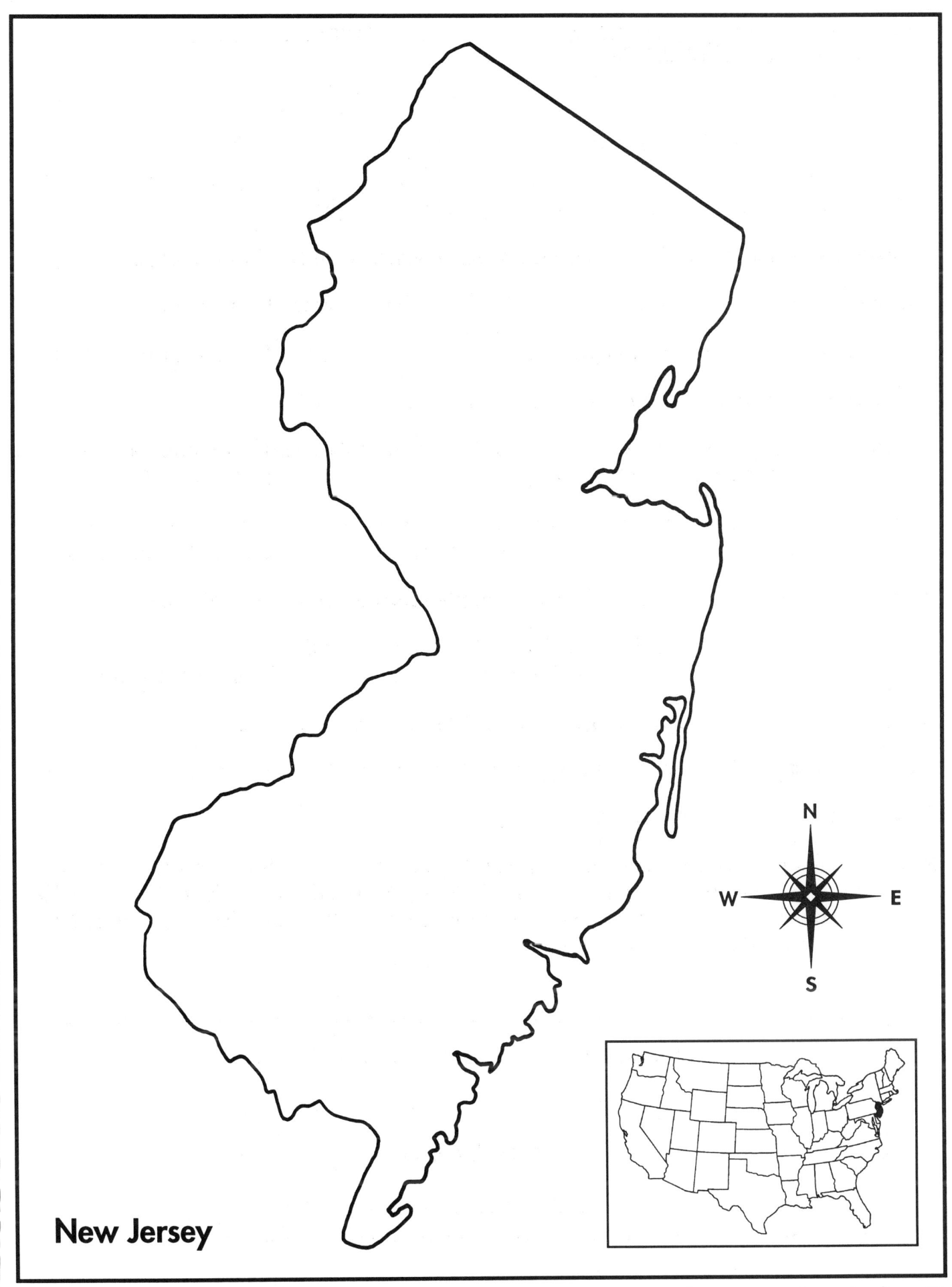

New Mexico

Land of Enchantment ❖ Sunshine State

Name _____

Date _____

First Non-Native American Settlement:

    The first Spanish colony in New Mexico was established in 1598, at the Pueblo of San Juan de Los Caballeros, near the Chama River. Santa Fe became the capital of the Mexican province in 1610 — making it the oldest seat of government in the entire United States.

Organized as a Territory: September 9, 1850.

Admitted to the Union: January 6, 1912 — the 47th state admitted into the Union.

Location: South-Central Region of the United States — part of the Southwestern States.

State Abbreviations: N. Mex. or N.M. (traditional use); NM (post office use).

Capital City: Santa Fe has been the capital since 1610, when New Mexico became part of the Spanish province of Mexico. San Gabriel was the capital from 1599 to 1610.

Land Area: 121,365 square miles. Ranks 5th in size among all of the 50 states. (2nd in size among the 4 Southwestern States.)

Population (1995 approximate): 1,600,000 people. Ranks 37th among all states.

    Density: 13 people per square mile.
    Distribution: 69% urban (city).   31% rural (non-city).

Largest City: Albuquerque — approximate population is 400,000 people.

Highest Elevation: Wheeler Peak — 13,161 feet above sea level.

State Motto: *"Crescit eundo."* (It grows as it goes.)

Important Historical Events: (a.) El Camino Real is the oldest road in the United States, running from Sante Fe to Chihuahua, Mexico. It first served travelers in 1581. Today it is Highway 81. (b.) The world's first atomic bomb was exploded on July 16, 1945, near Alamogordo. It was built at Los Alamos, New Mexico.

New Mexico's Animals ❖ Plants ❖ Symbols

Bird: Roadrunner   **Flower:** Yucca   **Tree:** Pinon

Gem: Turquoise   **Animal:** Black Bear   **Fish:** Cutthroat Trout

Colors: Red & Yellow of Old Spain   **Vegetables:** Chili & Frijol

Insect: Tarantula Hawk Wasp   **Cookie:** Bizcochito   **Grass:** Blue Gramma

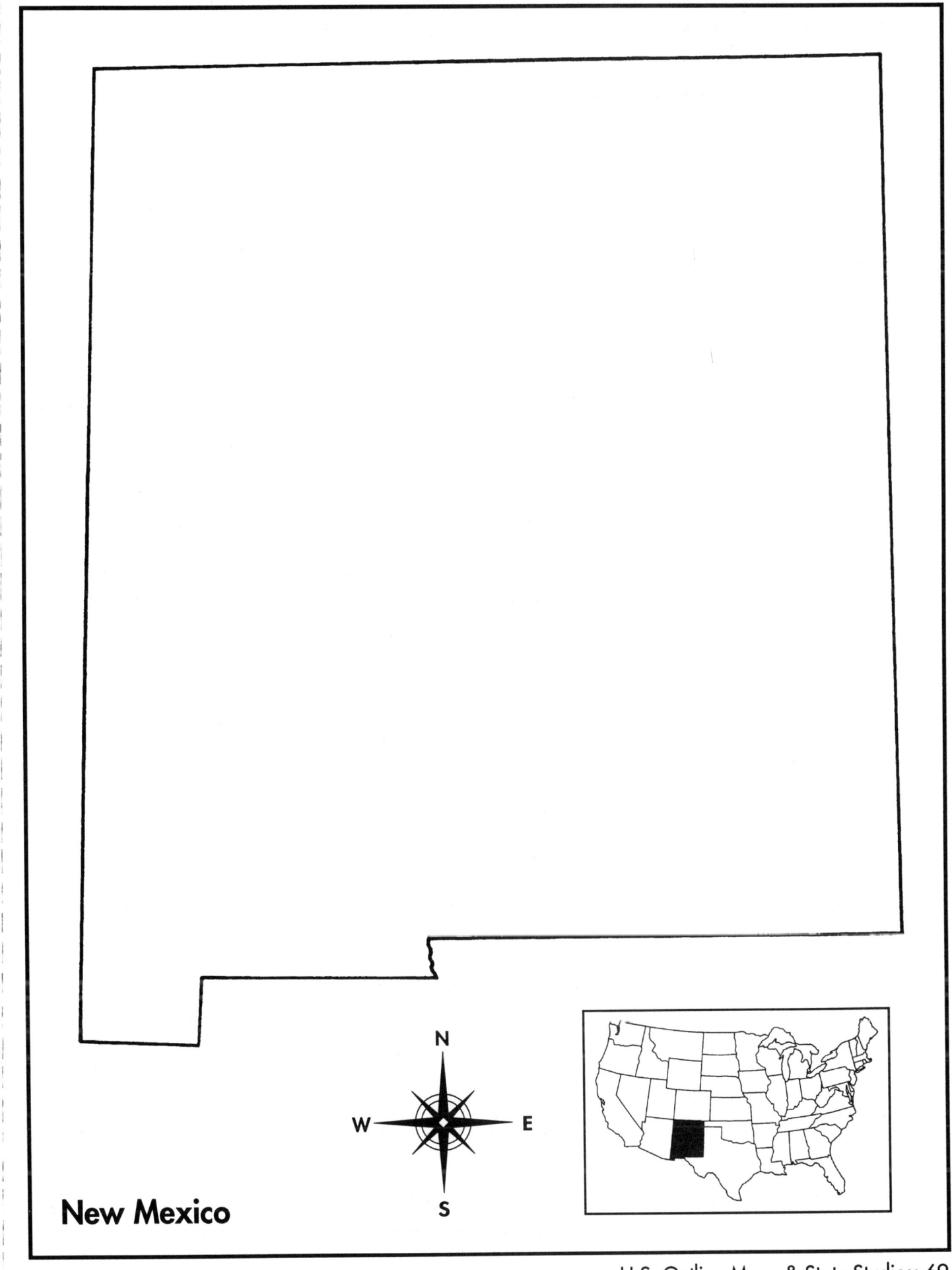

Empire State

Name _____

Date _____

First Non-Native American Settlement:
    In 1624, the Dutch established Fort Orange (today's Albany) as the first permanent white settlement in the New York region. A year later, more Dutch settlers began building New Amsterdam (today's New York City).

Organized as a Territory: New York was never a territory of the United States.

Admitted to the Union: July 26, 1788 — the 11th state admitted into the Union.

Location: Northeastern Region of the United States — part of the Middle Atlantic States.

State Abbreviations: N.Y. (traditional use); NY (post office use).

Capital City: Albany became the capital city in 1797. Kingston, Poughkeepsie, and New York City served as the capital between 1777 and 1797.

Land Area: 47,224 square miles.   Ranks 30th in size among all of the 50 states. (1st in size among the 3 Middle Atlantic States.)

Population (1995 approximate): 18,200,000 people. Ranks 2nd among all states.

    Density: 385 people per square mile.
    Distribution: 85% urban (city).   15% rural (non-city).

Largest City: New York — approximate population is 7,350,000 people.

Highest Elevation: Mt. Marcy — 5,344 feet above sea level.

State Motto: *"Excelsior."* (Ever Upward.)

Important Historical Events: (a.) In 1735, editor John Zenger was found innocent of libel, which was an important victory to keep "Freedom of the Press." He had criticized the British governor. (b.) The Erie Canal was completed in 1825, linking the Hudson River with the Great Lakes. This helped open the Midwest to settlers.

New York's Animals ❖ Plants ❖ Symbols

Bird: Bluebird	**Flower:** Rose	**Tree:** Sugar Maple
Insect: Ladybug	**Animal:** Beaver	**Fish:** Brook Trout
	Gem: Garnet	

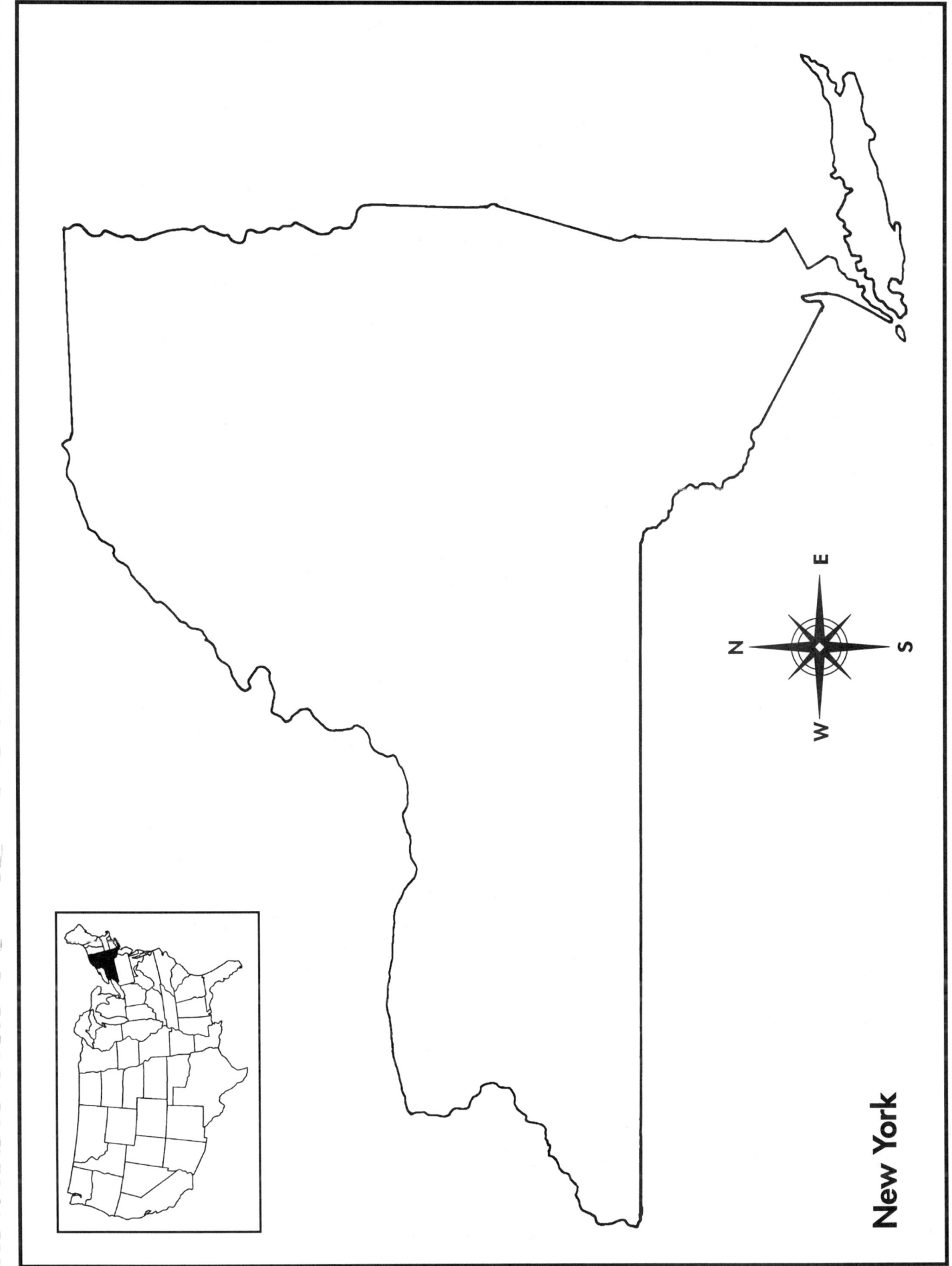

North Carolina

Tar Heel State

Name _____

Date _____

First Non-Native American Settlement:
In 1587, thirty-three years before the Pilgrims landed at Plymouth Rock, an English colony was founded on Roanoke Island. Three years later, a supply ship found no trace of the colony. Virginia Dare was the first child of English parents born in America. She was among the missing settlers.

Organized as a Territory: North Carolina was never a territory of the United States.

Admitted to the Union: November 21, 1789 — the 12th state admitted into the Union.

Location: Eastern-Central Region of the United States — part of the Southern States.

State Abbreviations: N.C. (traditional use); NC (post office use).

Capital City: Raleigh became the capital city in 1792. New Bern was the capital from 1771 to 1776. There was no official capital from 1776 to 1792.

Land Area: 48,718 square miles. Ranks 29th in size among all of the 50 states. (5th in size among the 14 Southern States.)

Population (1995 approximate): 7,000,000 people. Ranks 10th among all states.

Density: 175 people per square mile.
Distribution: 45% urban (city). 55% rural (non-city).

Largest City: Charlotte — approximate population is 400,000 people.

Highest Elevation: Mt. Mitchell — 6,684 feet above sea level.

State Motto: "Esse quam videri." (To be rather than to seem.)

Important Historical Event: The first successful airplane flight took place on December 17, 1903, at Kitty Hawk. The Wright brothers made a 12 second flight of 120 feet.

North Carolina's Animals ❖ Plants ❖ Symbols

Bird: Cardinal **Flower:** Dogwood **Gemstone:** Emerald **Tree:** Pine
Colors: Red & Blue **Mammal:** Gray Squirrel **Reptile:** Eastern Box Turtle
Rock: Granite **Dog:** Plott Hound **Beverage:** Milk
Shell: Scotch Bonnet **Historic Boat:** Shad Boat **Insect:** Honeybee

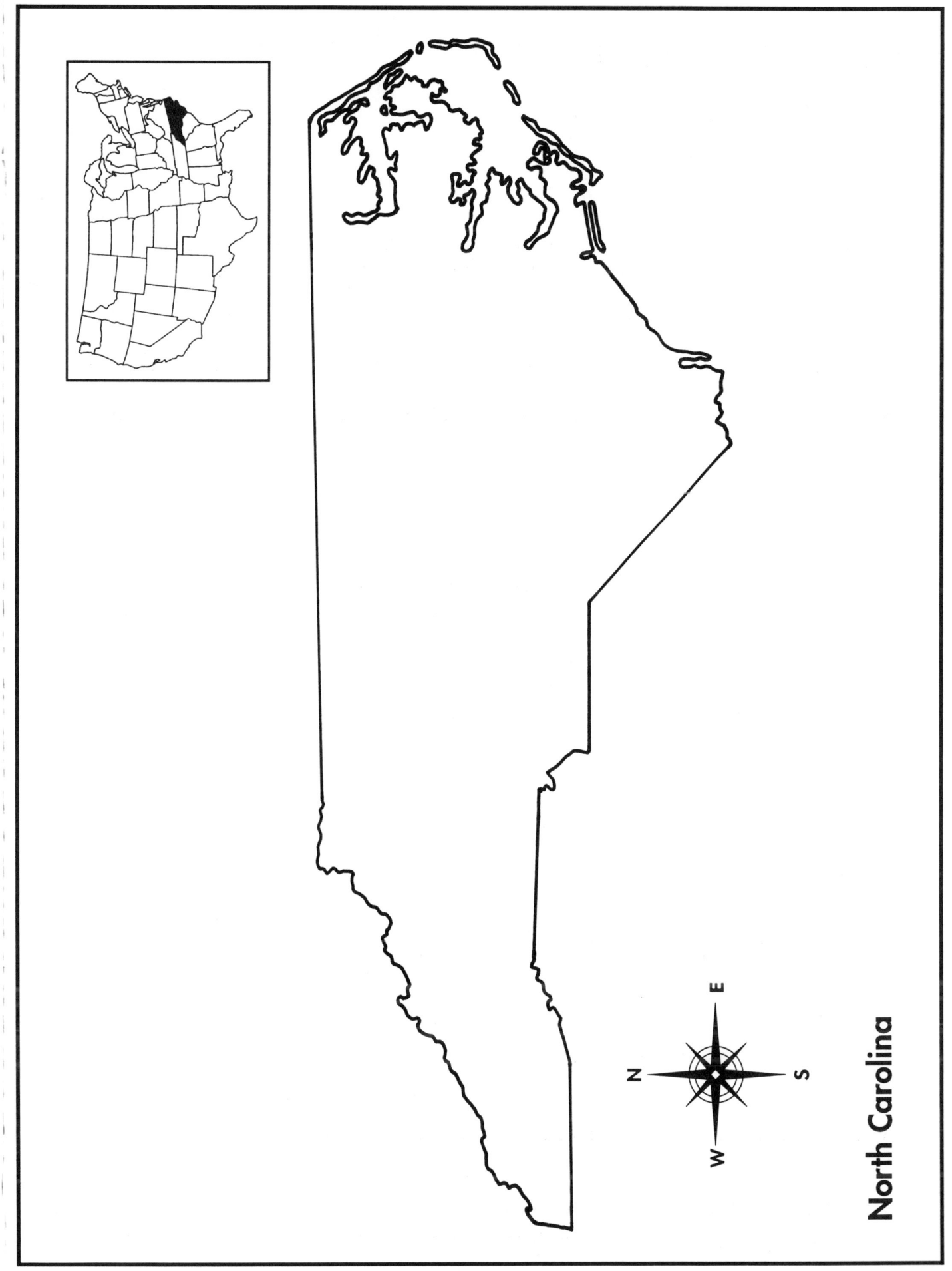

North Dakota

Sioux State ❖ *Flickertail State*
Peace Garden State

Name _____

Date _____

First Non-Native American Settlement:

In 1812, Scottish and Irish settlers made the first attempt at building a permanent settlement in the area of today's North Dakota. They built it at the location of Pembina.

Organized as a Territory: March 2, 1861.

Admitted to the Union: November 2, 1889 — the 39th state admitted into the Union.

Location: North-Central Region of the United States — part of the Midwestern States.

State Abbreviations: N.Dak. or N.D. (traditional use); ND (post office use).

Capital City: Bismarck has been the capital since North Dakota became a state in 1889.

Land Area: 68,994 square miles. Ranks 17th in size among all of the 50 states. (5th in size among the 12 Midwestern States.)

Population (1995 approximate): 650,000 people. Ranks 47th among all states.

Density: 9 people per square mile.
Distribution: 44% urban (city). 56% rural (non-city).

Largest City: Fargo — approximate population is 74,250 people.

Highest Elevation: White Butte — 3,506 feet above sea level.

State Motto: "Liberty and Union, Now and Forever: One and Inseparable."

Important Historical Event: Raising wheat boosted North Dakota's agriculture industry in the 1870's. The crop was grown on large "bonanza farms." North Dakota leads the rest of the states in durum* wheat production. (***Durum** is a hard wheat that produces flour and semolina used in macaroni, spaghetti and other types of noodles.)

North Dakota's Animals ❖ Plants ❖ Symbols

Bird: Western Meadowlark   **Tree:** American Elm

Flower: Wild Prairie Rose

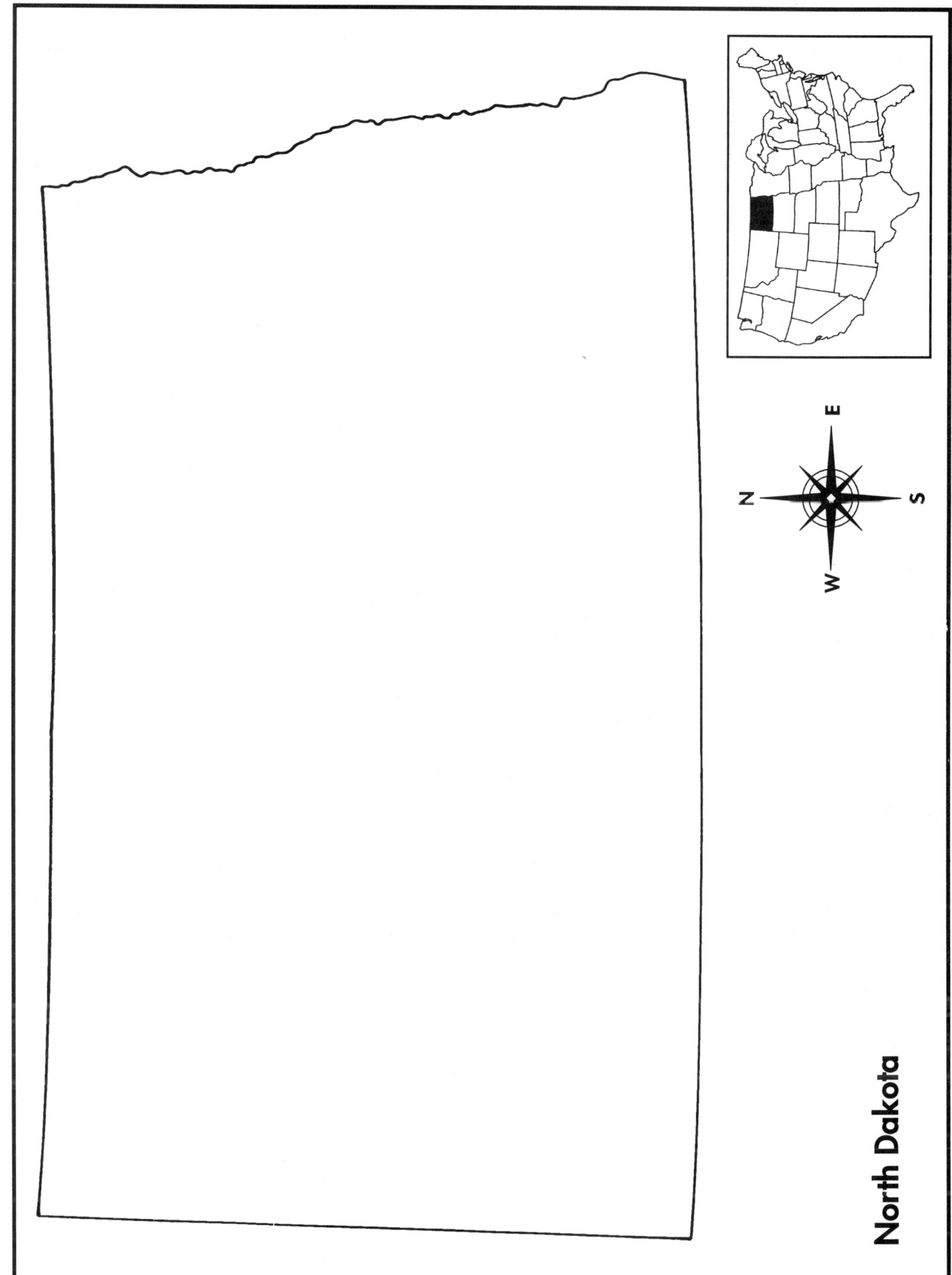

Ohio
Buckeye State

Name _____

Date _____

First Non-Native American Settlement:
    The first permanent white settlement in Ohio was established in April of 1788, by General Rufus Putnam. Putnam is sometimes called the "Father of Ohio." This settlement is now the city of Marietta.

Organized as a Territory: Ohio was never a territory of the United States.

Admitted to the Union: March 1, 1803 — the 17th state admitted into the Union.

Location: Northeastern Region of the United States — part of the Midwestern States.

State Abbreviations: O. (traditional use); OH (post office use).

Capital City: Columbus has been the capital city since 1816. Other capitals were Chillicothe (1803-1810 and 1812-1816) and Zanesville (1810-1812).

Land Area: 40,953 square miles.   Ranks 35th in size among all of the 50 states. (11th in size among the 12 Midwestern States.)

Population (1995 approximate): 11,100,000 people. Ranks 7th among all states.

    Density: 271 people per square mile.
    Distribution: 75% urban (city).   25% rural (non-city).

Largest City: Columbus — approximate population is 640,000 people.

Highest Elevation: Campbell Hill — 1,550 feet above sea level.

State Motto: "With God, all things are possible."

Important Historical Event: In 1870, B.F. Goodrich began making rubber fire hoses, as well as other rubber products, in Akron. Later, in 1895, the first pneumatic tire was used, and Akron helped get the world riding on rubber tires.

Ohio's Animals ❖ Plants ❖ Symbols

Flower: Scarlet Carnation   **Tree:** Buckeye

Bird: Cardinal   **Insect:** Ladybug

Gemstone: Flint   **Drink:** Tomato Juice

Sooner State

Name _____

Date _____

First Non-Native American Settlement:
The first white settlements were established at Miller Court House (in present-day McCurtain County), Salina and Three Forks in about 1819. In 1824, the U.S. Army built Fort Towson and Fort Gibson.

Organized as a Territory: May 2, 1890.

Admitted to the Union: November 16, 1907 — the 46th state admitted into the Union.

Location: Central Region of the United States — part of the Southwestern States.

State Abbreviations: Okla. (traditional use); OK (post office use).

Capital City: Oklahoma City has been the capital city since 1910. The only other capital was Guthrie from 1890-1910.

Land Area: 68,679 square miles.   Ranks 19th in size among all of the 50 states. (4th in size among the 4 Southwestern States.)

Population (1995 approximate): 3,250,000 people. Ranks 28th among all states.

   Density: 47 people per square mile.
   Distribution: 68% urban (city).   32% rural (non-city).

Largest City: Oklahoma City — approximate population is 450,000 people.

Highest Elevation: Black Mesa — 4,973 feet above sea level.

State Motto: "Labor omnia vincit." (Labor conquers all things.)

Important Historical Event: After Forts Gibson and Towson were built in 1824, the U.S. government forced the Cherokee, Chickasaw, Choctaw, Creek, and Seminole Indian nations off their respective lands.

Oklahoma's Animals ❖ Plants ❖ Symbols

Flower: Mistletoe   **Stone:** Rose Rock (barite rose)

Colors: Green & White   **Bird:** Scissor-tailed Flycatcher

Animal: Bison   **Reptile:** Mountain Boomer Lizard   **Tree:** Redbud

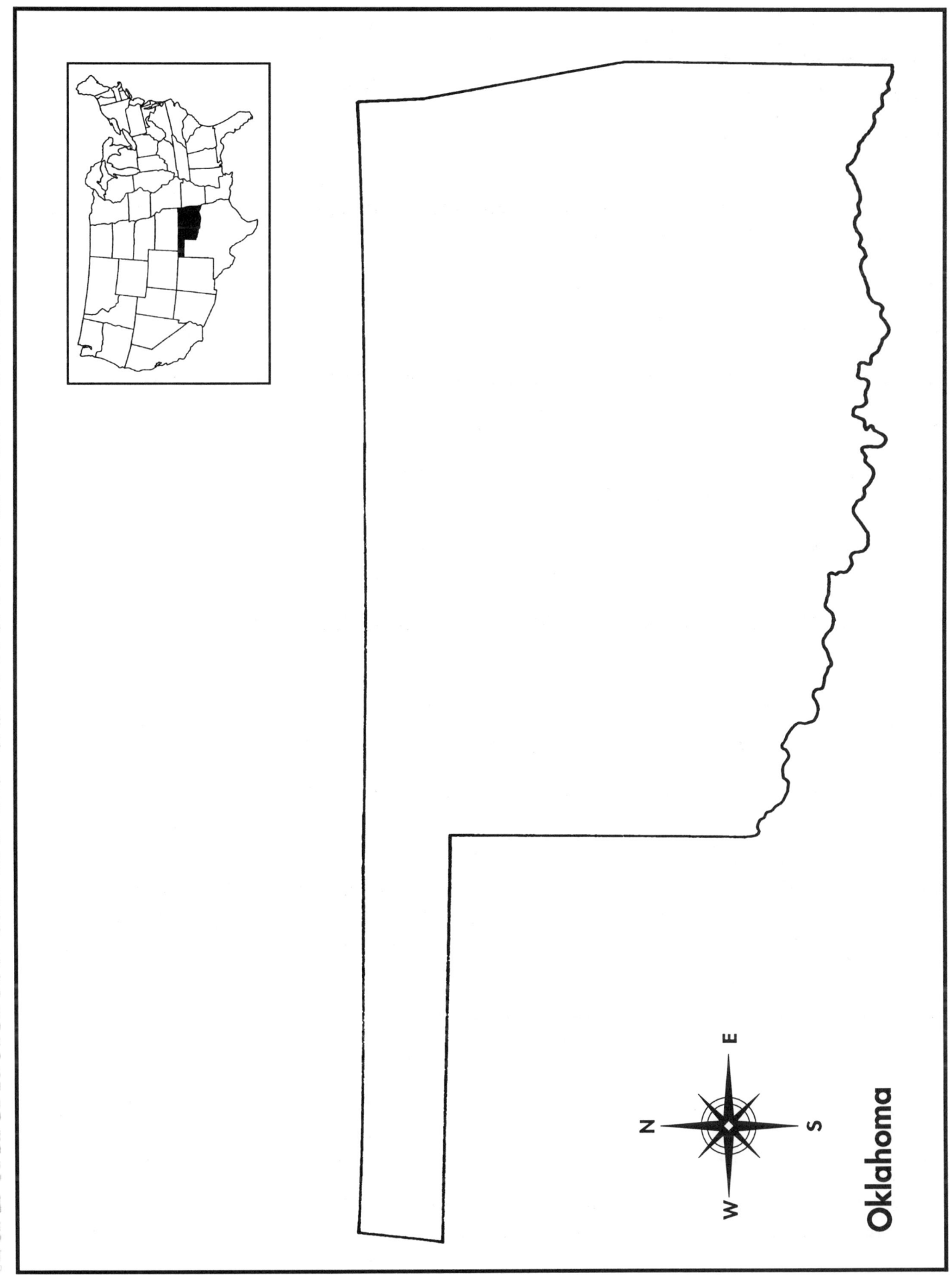

Beaver State

Name _____

Date _____

First Non-Native American Settlement:
    The settlement of Astoria was founded by John Jacob Astor's American Fur Company in 1811. It was Oregon's first settlement. In 1834, Methodist missionaries established the first permanent American settlement in the Willamette Valley.

Organized as a Territory: August 14, 1848.

Admitted to the Union: February 14, 1859 — the 33rd state admitted into the Union.

Location: Northwestern Region of the United States — part of the Pacific Coast States.

State Abbreviations: Ore. (traditional use); OR (post office use).

Capital City: Salem has been the capital city since 1855. The other capitals were Oregon City (1849-1851), Salem (1851-1855) and Corvallis (1855).

Land Area: 96,003 square miles.   Ranks 10th in size among all of the 50 states. (2nd in size among the 3 Pacific Coast States.)

Population (1995 approximate)**:** 3,000,000 people. Ranks 29th among all states.

    Density: 31 people per square mile.
    Distribution: 67% urban (city).   33% rural (non-city).

Largest City: Portland — approximate population is 450,000 people.

Highest Elevation: Mt. Hood — 11,235 feet above sea level.

State Motto: "Alis volat Propriis." (She flies with her own wings.)

Important Historical Event: In 1877, the great Chief Joseph led the Nez Percé Indians in a war against the white settlers and armies that were attempting to take the tribe's land. This was one of the last efforts of the Northwestern Indians to try to keep their lifestyle, customs and heritage free of the white settlers' influence.

Oregon's Animals ❖ Plants ❖ Symbols

Rock: Thunderegg	**Flower:** Oregon Grape	**Tree:** Douglas Fir
Colors: Navy Blue & Gold	**Animal:** Beaver	**Fish:** Chinook Salmon
	Bird: Western Meadowlark	

U.S. Outline Maps & State Studies: 80   © Golden Educational Center

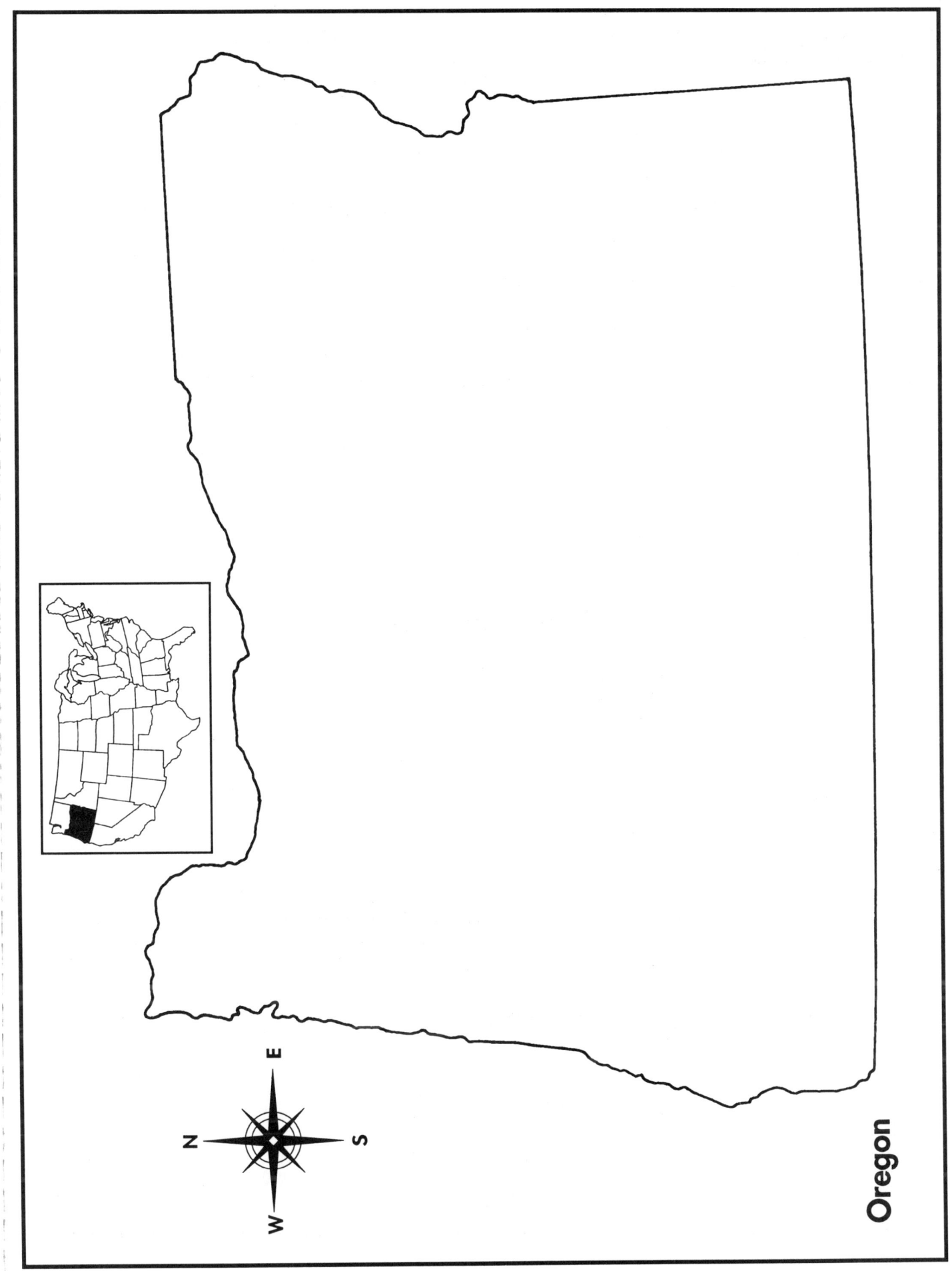

Pennsylvania

Keystone State

Name _____

Date _____

First Non-Native American Settlement:

    In 1643, the Swedes established the first permanent white settlement in Pennsylvania. They made Tinicum Island, near today's Philadelphia, the capital of their colony named New Sweden. King Charles II gave the Pennsylvania region to William Penn in 1681.

Organized as a Territory: Pennsylvania was never a territory of the United States.

Admitted to the Union: December 12, 1787 — the 2nd state admitted into the Union.

Location: Northeastern Region of the United States — part of the Middle Atlantic States.

State Abbreviations: Pa. or Penn. (traditional use); PA (post office use).

Capital City: Harrisburg became the capital city in 1812. Other capitals were Chester (1681-1683), Philadelphia (1683-1799) and Lancaster (1799-1812).

Land Area: 44,820 square miles. Ranks 32nd in size among all of the 50 states. (2nd in size among the Middle Atlantic States.)

Population (1995 approximate): 12,030,000 people. Ranks 5th among all states.

    Density: 268 people per square mile.
    Distribution: 71% urban (city).   29% rural (non-city).

Largest City: Philadelphia — approximate population is 1,600,000 people.

Highest Elevation: Mt. Davis — 3,213 feet above sea level.

State Motto: "Virtue, Liberty & Independence."

Important Historical Events: (a.) The *Declaration of Independence*, proclaiming the freedom of the 13 colonies from English rule was signed in Philadelphia in 1776.
(b.) The "Constitution of the United States" was adopted and signed in Philadelphia on September 17, 1787.

Pennsylvania's Animals ❖ Plants ❖ Symbols

Bird: Ruffed Grouse   **Flower:** Mountain Laurel   **Tree:** Hemlock

Colors: Blue & Gold   **Dog:** Great Dane

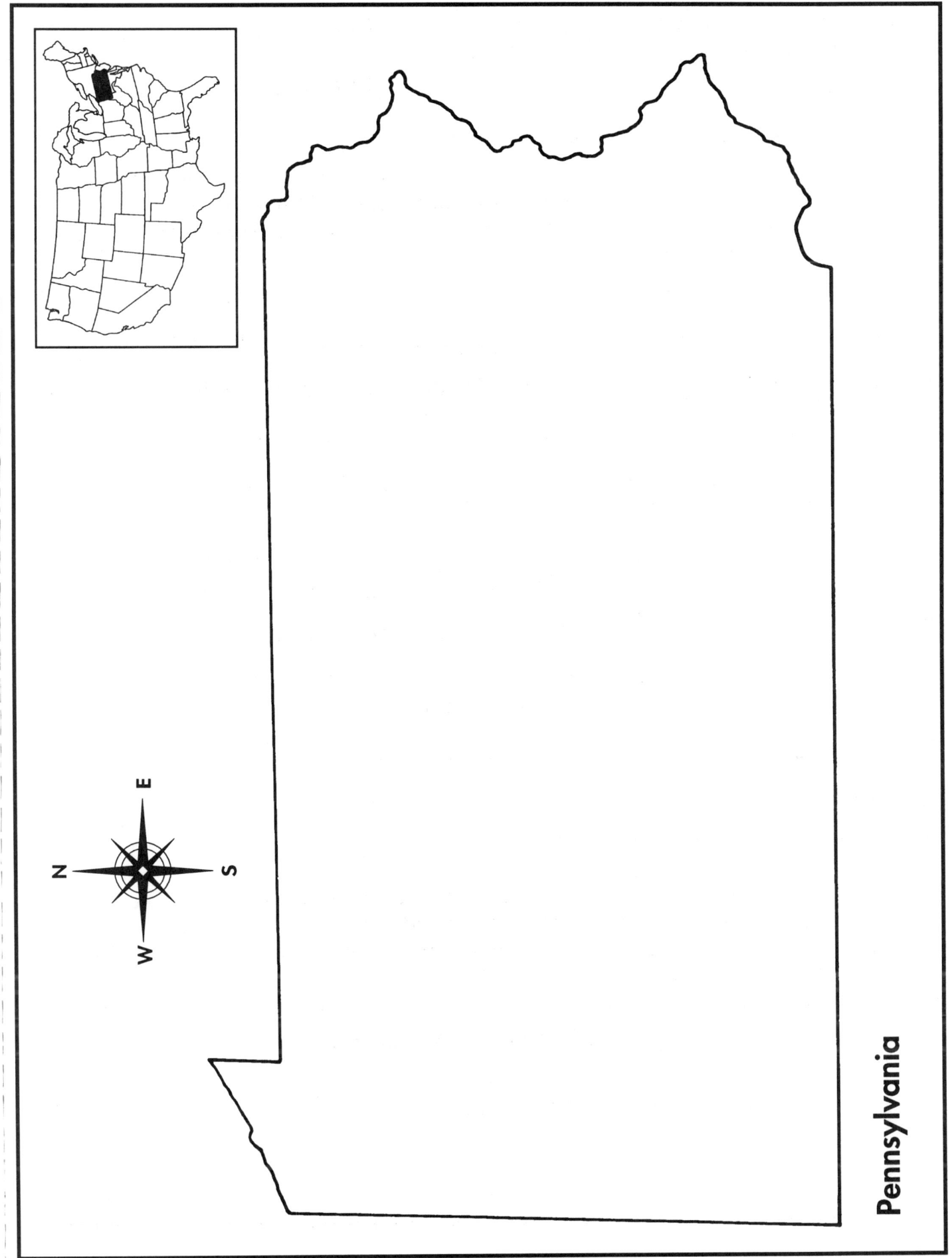

Rhode Island

The Ocean State

Name _____

Date _____

First Non-Native American Settlement:
In 1636, Roger Williams established Rhode Island's first permanent white settlement, at Providence.

Organized as a Territory: Rhode Island was never a territory of the United States.

Admitted to the Union: May 29, 1790 — the 13th state admitted into the Union.

Location: Northeastern Region of the United States — part of the New England States.

State Abbreviations: R.I. (traditional use); RI (post office use).

Capital City: Providence became the capital city in 1900. Earlier capitals from 1663 to 1900 were Newport, East Greenwich, Bristol, South Kingston and Providence.

Land Area: 1,045 square miles.   Ranks 50th in size among all of the 50 states. (6th in size among the 6 New England States.)

Population (1995 approximate): 1,007,000 people. Ranks 43rd among all states.

Density: 960 people per square mile.
Distribution: 87% urban (city).   13% rural (non-city).

Largest City: Providence — approximate population is 161,000 people.

Highest Elevation: Jerimoth Hill — 812 feet above sea level.

State Motto: "Hope."

Important Historical Events: (a.) Slave traders brought thousands of slaves to Rhode Island ports until 1774, when the colonies prohibited the importation of slaves. (b.) The Slater Mill was one of North America's first successful textile mills. It was built in Pawtucket in 1793.

Rhode Island's Animals ❖ Plants ❖ Symbols

Bird: Rhode Island Red   **Flower:** Violet (Unofficial)

Shell: Quahog   **Colors:** Blue, White & Gold   **Tree:** Red Maple

Stone: Cumberlandite   **Mineral:** Bowenite

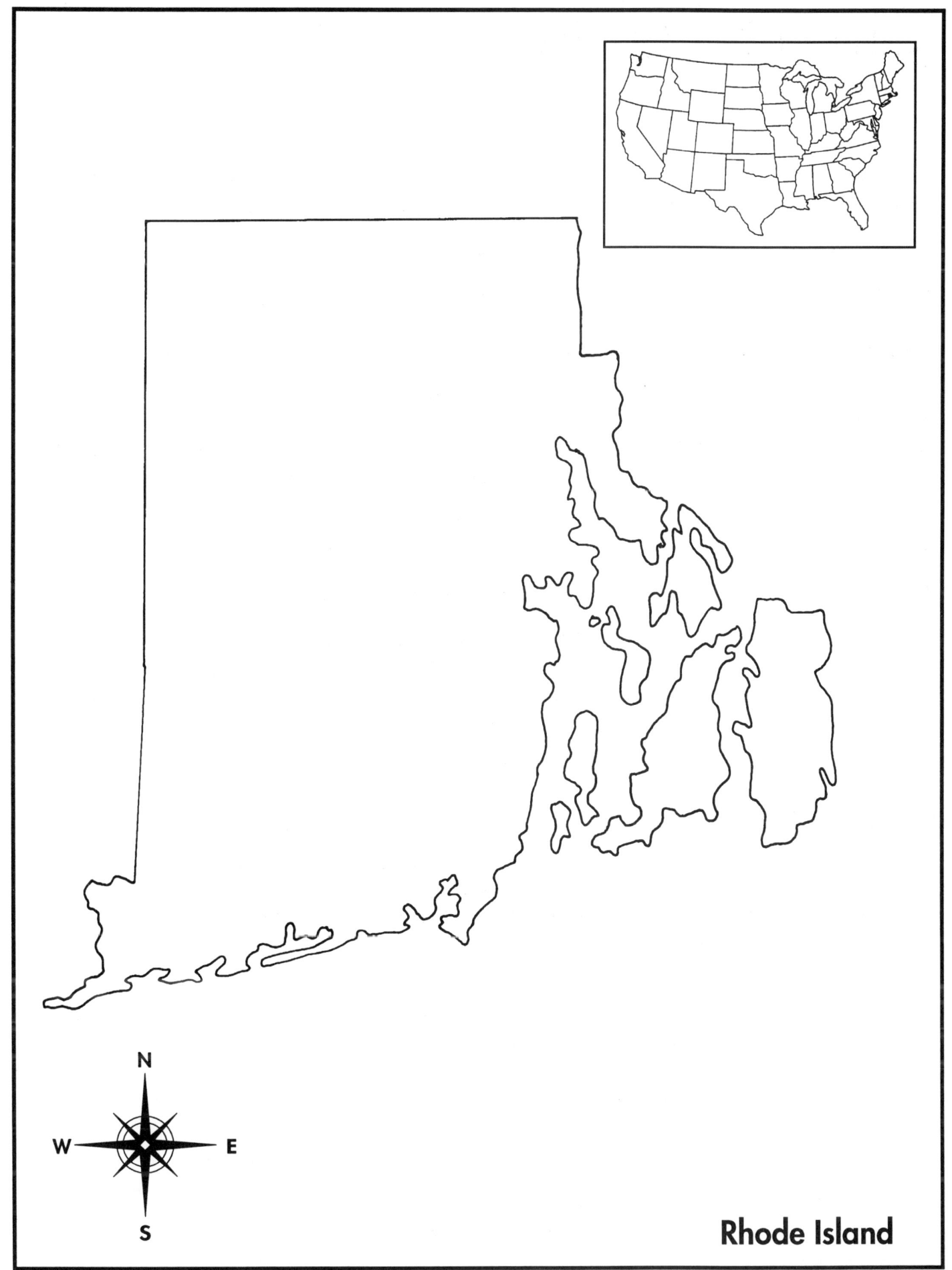

South Carolina

Palmetto State

Name _____

Date _____

First Non-Native American Settlement:
 In 1670, the first English settlers arrived at Albemarle Point, near what is now Charleston, South Carolina. There they established the first white settlement in the area. In 1680, they moved the settlement to Oyster Point and named it "Charles Town."

Organized as a Territory: South Carolina was never a territory of the United States.

Admitted to the Union: May 23, 1788 — the 8th state admitted into the Union.

Location: Southeastern Coast Region of the United States — part of the Southern States.

State Abbreviations: S.C. (traditional use); SC (post office use).

Capital City: Columbia became the capital city in 1790. The only other capital was Charleston from 1670 to 1790.

Land Area: 30,111 square miles. Ranks 40th in size among all of the 50 states. (11th in size among the 14 Southern States.)

Population (1995 approximate): 3,650,000 people. Ranks 25th among all states.

 Density: 121 people per square mile.
 Distribution: 48% urban (city). 52% rural (non-city).

Largest City: Columbia — approximate population is 100,000 people.

Highest Elevation: Sassafras Mountain — 3,560 feet above sea level.

State Mottos: "Prepared in mind and resources." & "While I breathe, I hope."

Important Historical Events: (a.) The nation's first opera performance, about 1702; (b.) one of the nation's first museums, founded in 1773; (c.) the first fireproof building, built in 1822; and (d.) the first steam locomotive in service, 1830.

South Carolina's Animals ❖ Plants ❖ Symbols

Flower: Carolina Yellow Jessamine

Bird: Carolina Wren

Tree: Palmetto

U.S. Outline Maps & State Studies: 86

© Golden Educational Center

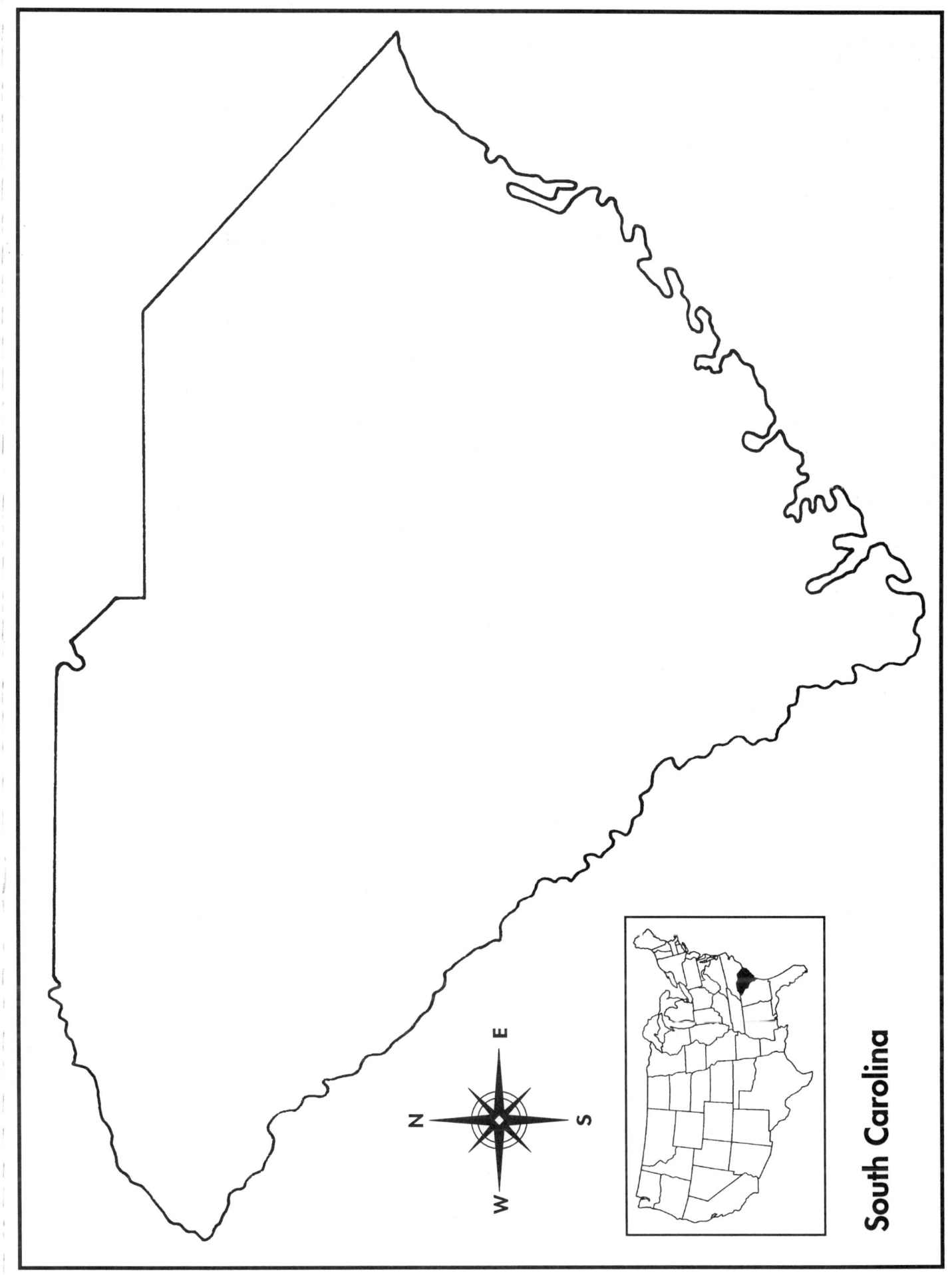

South Dakota

Mount Rushmore State ❖ Coyote State

Name _____

Date _____

First Non-Native American Settlement:
    Joseph La Framboise, a French fur trader, established the first settlement in South Dakota in 1817. The settlement was located at the site of present-day Fort Pierre, at the junction of the Missouri and Bad Rivers.

Organized as a Territory: March 2, 1861.

Admitted to the Union: November 2, 1889 — the 40th state admitted into the Union.

Location: North-Central Region of the United States — part of the Midwestern States.

State Abbreviations: S.Dak. or S.D. (traditional use); SD (post office use).

Capital City: Pierre has been the capital city since 1889. Other capitals were Yankton (1861-1883) and Bismarck (1883-1889).

Land Area: 75,898 square miles. Ranks 16th in size among all of the 50 states. (4th in size among the 12 Midwestern States.)

Population (1995 approximate): 700,000 people. Ranks 45th among all states.

    Density: 9 people per square mile.
    Distribution: 46% urban (city). 54% rural (non-city).

Largest City: Sioux Falls — approximate population 101,000 people.

Highest Elevation: Harney Peak — 7,242 feet above sea level.

State Motto: "Under God the people rule."

Important Historical Event: In 1927, Gutzon Borglum began work on Mount Rushmore National Memorial. It took over 14 years for him to complete the 465 feet high sculpted heads of Presidents Washington, Jefferson, T. Roosevelt and Lincoln.

South Dakota's Animals ❖ Plants ❖ Symbols

Flower: American Pasqueflower   **Tree:** Black Hills Spruce
Colors: Blue & Gold   **Bird:** Ringnecked Pheasant   **Animal:** Coyote
Grass: Western Wheat   **Soil:** Houdek   **Insect:** Honeybee
Mineral Stone: Rose Quartz   **Gem:** Fairburn Agate   **Fish:** Walleye

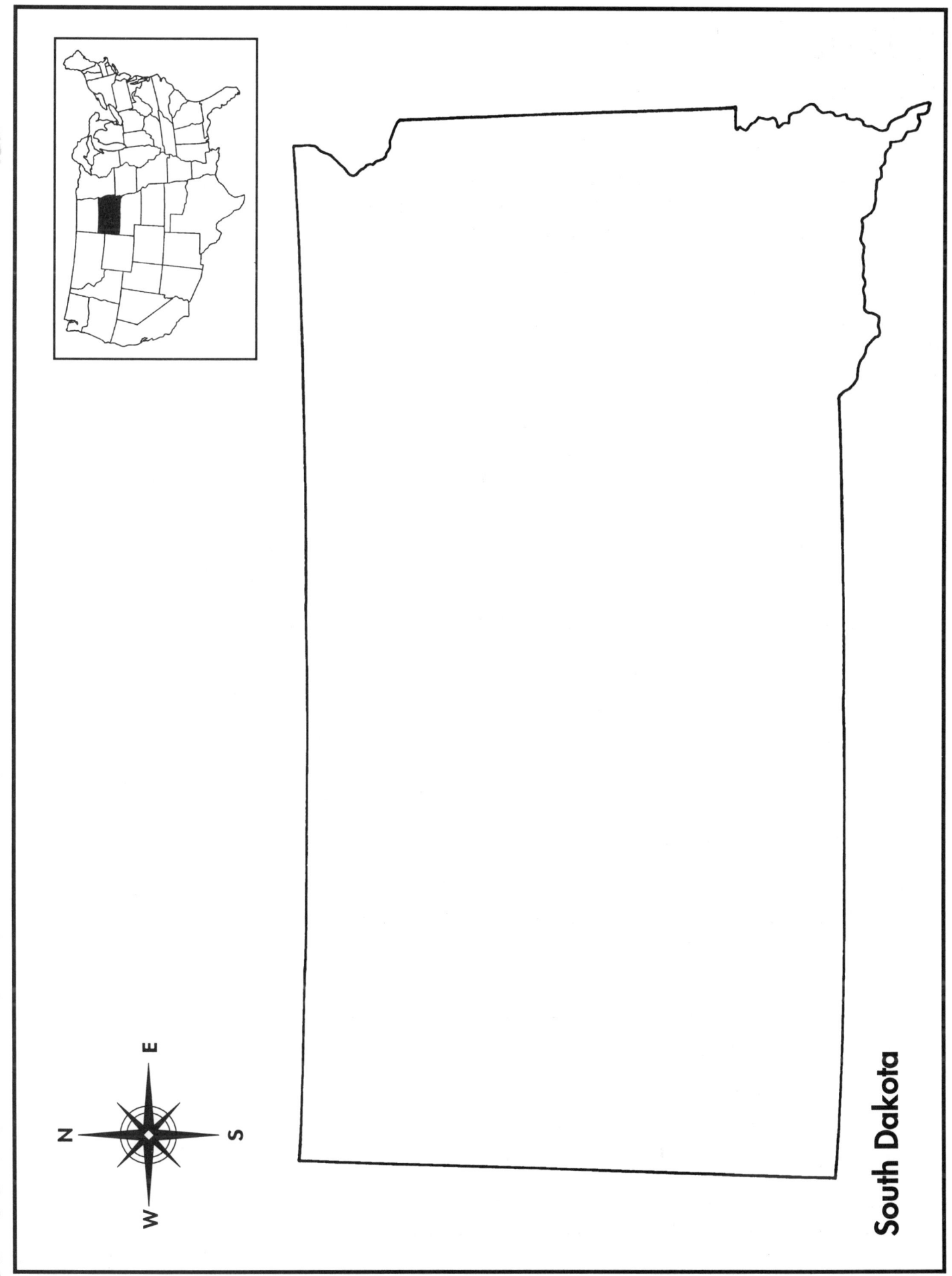

Tennessee
Volunteer State

Name _____

Date _____

First Non-Native American Settlement:
    In 1714, French settlers started moving into the region where Nashville is today. Charles Charlesville built a French trading post at French Lick.

Organized as a Territory: Tennessee was never a territory of the United States.

Admitted to the Union: June 1, 1796 — the 16th state admitted into the Union.

Location: Eastern-Central Region of the United States — part of the Southern States.

State Abbreviations: Tenn. (traditional use); TN (post office use).

Capital City: Nashville became the capital city in 1826. It was also the capital from 1812 to 1817. Other capitals were Knoxville (1792-1812 and 1817) and Murfreesboro from 1818 to 1826.

Land Area: 41,220 square miles. Ranks 34th in size among all of the 50 states. (8th in size among the 14 Southern States.)

Population (1995 approximate): 5,150,000 people. Ranks 18th among all states.

    Density: 124 people per square mile.
    Distribution: 59% urban (city).   41% rural (non-city).

Largest City: Memphis — approximate population is 625,000 people.

Highest Elevation: Clingmans Dome — 6,643 feet above sea level.

State Motto: "Agriculture & Commerce." (1987) "Tennessee, America at its best!" (1965)

Important Historical Event: Tennessee was the last state to join the South in the Civil War (June 8, 1861). It was the first state to be readmitted to the Union after the Civil War ended (1865).

Tennessee's Animals ❖ Plants ❖ Symbols

Wild Flower: Passion Flower   **Flower:** Iris

Bird: Mockingbird   **Horse:** Tennessee Walking   **Animal:** Raccoon

Tree: Tulip Poplar

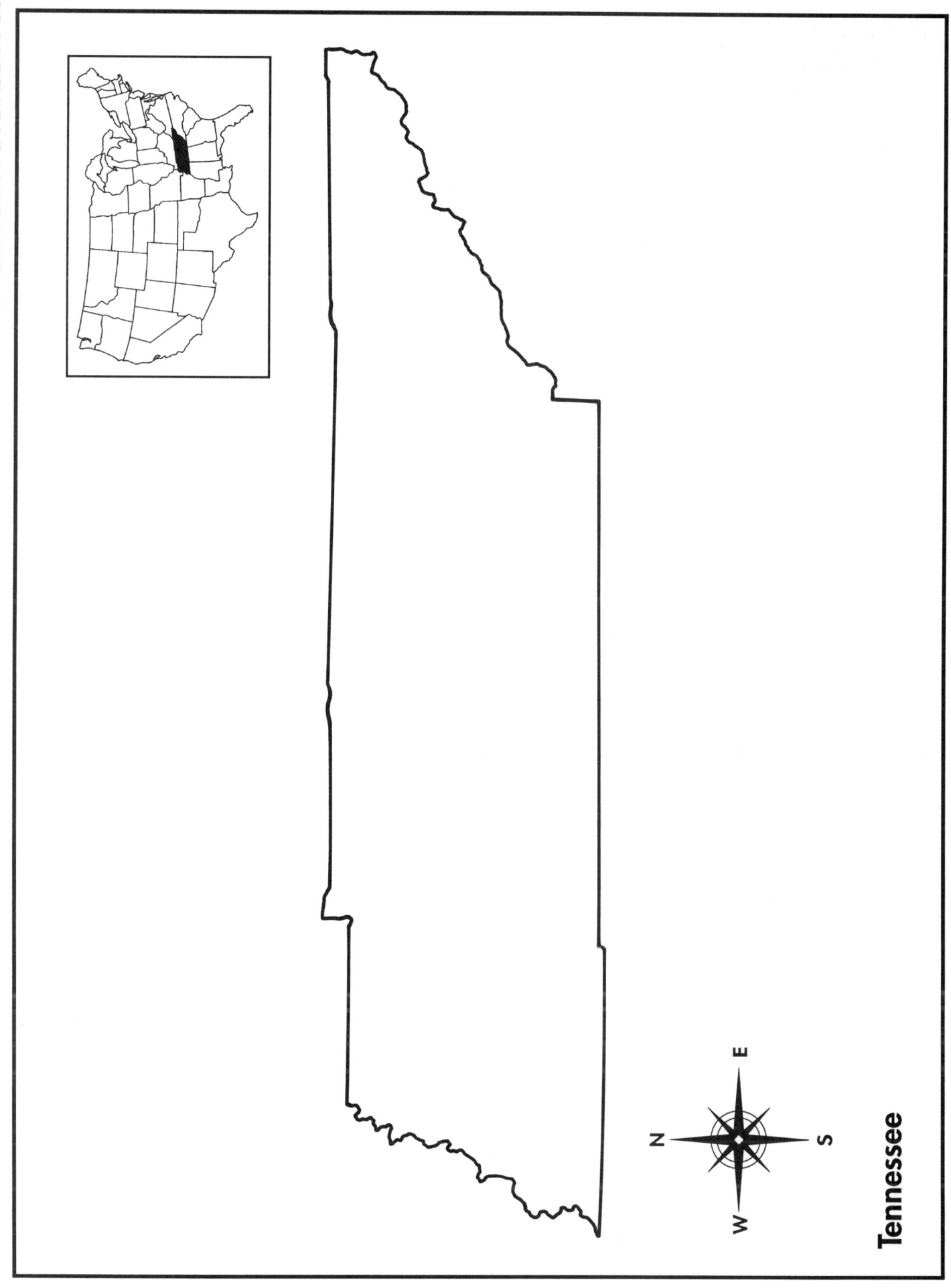

Texas
Lone Star State

Name _____

Date _____

First Non-Native American Settlement:
    In 1682, Spanish missionaries established the first two missions in Texas. These missions were built near present-day El Paso. In 1821, the first colony of Americans settled at Washington-on-the-Brazos and Columbus in southeast Texas.

Organized as a Territory: Texas was never a territory of the United States.

Admitted to the Union: December 29, 1845 — the 28th state admitted into the Union.

Location: South-Central Region of the United States — part of the Southwestern States.

State Abbreviations: Tex. (traditional use); TX (post office use).

Capital City: Austin has been the capital city since 1845. Other capitals were Houston (1837-1840), Austin (1840-1842) and Washington-on-the-Brazos (1842-1845).

Land Area: 261,914 square miles. Ranks 2nd in size among all of the 50 states. (1st in size among the 4 Southwestern States.)

Population (1995 approximate): 17,800,000 people. Ranks 3rd among all states.

       Density: 68 people per square mile.
       Distribution: 80% urban (city).   20% rural (non-city).

Largest City: Houston — approximate population is 1,700,000 people.

Highest Elevation: Guadalupe Peak — 8,751 feet above sea level.

State Motto: "Friendship."

Important Historical Events: (a.) In 1962, construction began on the Manned Spacecraft Center in Houston. (b.) President John F. Kennedy was assassinated in Dallas on November 22, 1963.

Texas' Animals ❖ Plants ❖ Symbols

Bird: Mockingbird   **Flower:** Bluebonnet   **Tree:** Pecan

Seashell: Lightning Whelk   **Fish:** Guadalupe Bass

U.S. Outline Maps & State Studies: 92   © Golden Educational Center

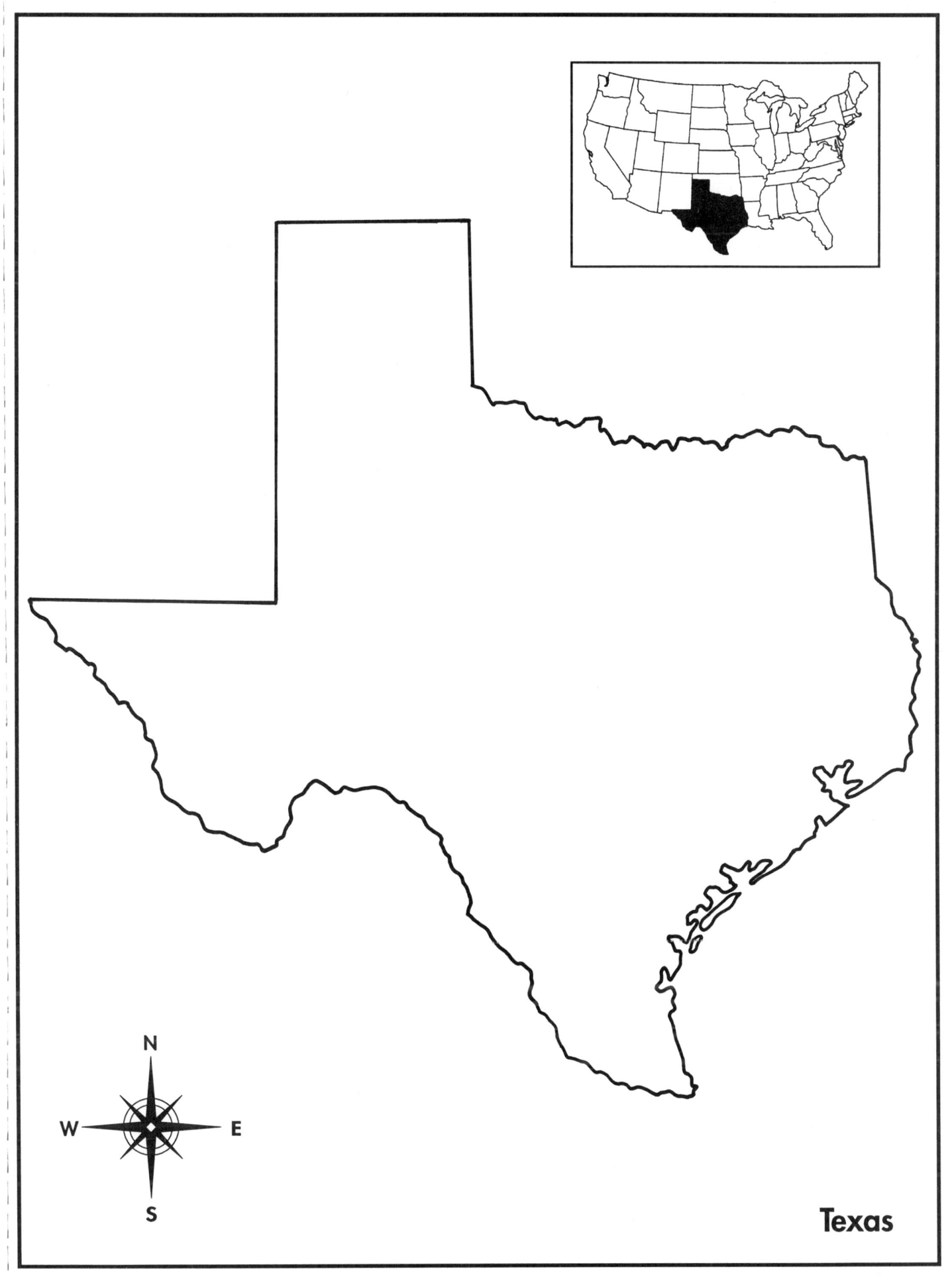

Beehive State

Name _____

Date _____

First Non-Native American Settlement:
 The Mormons were the first permanent settlers in the Utah region. Brigham Young, the Mormon leader, came to the Salt Lake Valley on July 24, 1847.

Organized as a Territory: September 9, 1850.

Admitted to the Union: January 4, 1896 — the 45th state admitted into the Union.

Location: Western-Central Region of the U.S. — part of the Rocky Mountain States.

State Abbreviations: Ut. (traditional use); UT (post office use).

Capital City: Salt Lake City became the capital city in 1856. Fillmore was the capital from 1851 to 1856.

Land Area: 82,168 square miles.   Ranks 12th in size among all of the 50 states. (6th in size among the 6 Rocky Mountain States.)

Population (1995 approximate): 1,850,000 people. Ranks 35th among all states.

   Density: 23 people per square mile.
   Distribution: 84% urban (city).   16% rural (non-city).

Largest City: Salt Lake City — approximate population is 165,000 people.

Highest Elevation: Kings Peak — 13,528 feet above sea level.

State Motto: "Industry."

Important Historical Event: The first United States Transcontinental Railroad System was completed at Promontory, Utah, on May 10, 1869. This railroad system linked the Central Pacific (from Sacramento, California) and the Union Pacific (from Omaha, Nebraska).

Utah's Animals ❖ Plants ❖ Symbols

Bird: Seagull   **Flower:** Sego Lily   **Tree:** Blue Spruce

Emblem: Beehive

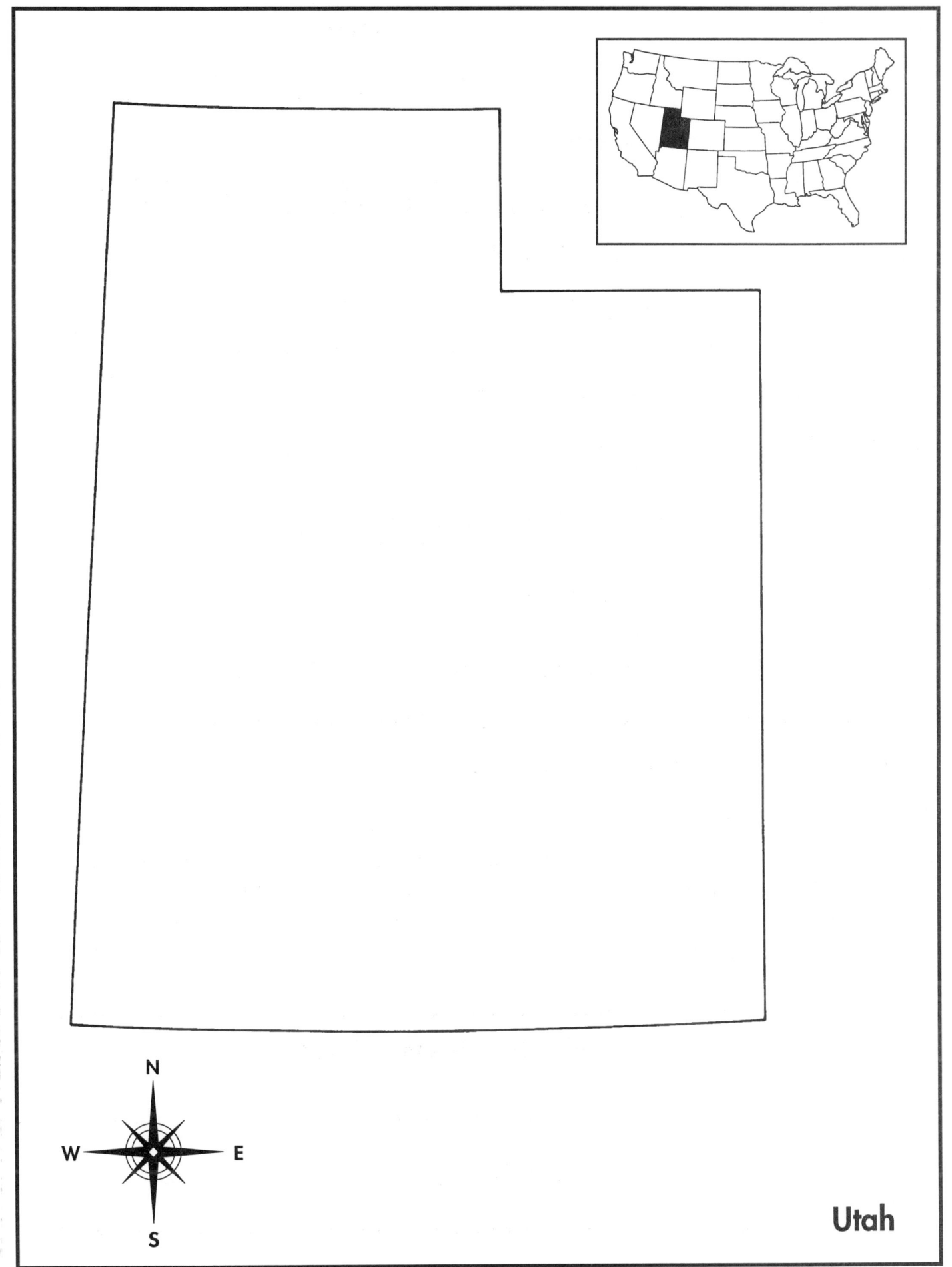

Green Mountain State

Name _____

Date _____

First Non-Native American Settlement:

    Fort Dummer was the first white settlement in Vermont. It was built in 1724, near what is now Brattleboro. It was built to protect western settlements from French raids.

Organized as a Territory: Vermont was never a territory of the United States.

Admitted to the Union: March 4, 1791 — the 14th state admitted into the Union.

Location: Northeastern Region of the United States — part of the New England States.

State Abbreviations: Vt. (traditional use); VT (post office use).

Capital City: Montpelier became the capital in 1805. Many other towns served as temporary capitals from 1777 to 1805.

Land Area: 9,249 square miles.   Ranks 43rd in size among all of the 50 states. (2nd in size among the 6 New England States.)

Population (1995 approximate)**:** 610,000 people. Ranks 48th among all states.

    Density: 62 people per square mile.
    Distribution: 32% urban (city).   68% rural (non-city).

Largest City: Burlington — approximate population is 40,000 people.

Highest Elevation: Mt. Mansfield — 4,393 feet above sea level.

State Motto: "Freedom & Unity."

Important Historical Event: Vermont joined the United States on March 4, 1791, making it the first territory to become a state after the original 13 colonies formed the United States.

Vermont's Animals ❖ Plants ❖ Symbols

Bird: Hermit Thrush   **Flower:** Red Clover   **Tree:** Sugar Maple

Animal: Morgan Horse   **Insect:** Honeybee

U.S. Outline Maps & State Studies: 96   © Golden Educational Center

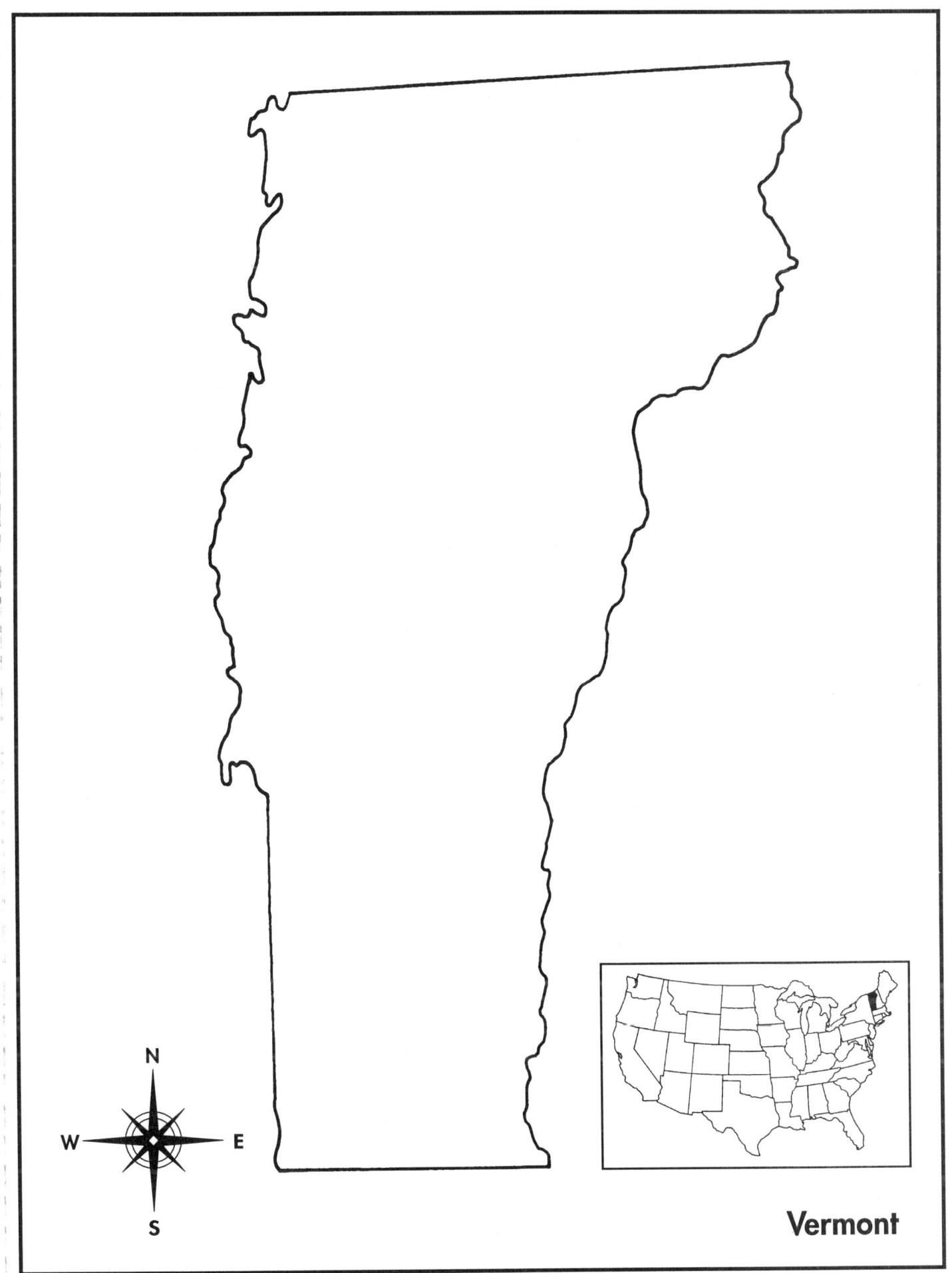

Virginia

Old Dominion ❖ Mother of Presidents

Name _____

Date _____

First Non-Native American Settlement:
America's first permanent English settlement was in 1607. It was located in the region that would become Virginia. The name of this settlement was Jamestown.

Organized as a Territory: Virginia was never a territory of the United States.

Admitted to the Union: June 25, 1788 — the 10th state admitted into the Union.

Location: Eastern-Central Coast Region of the U.S. — part of the Southern States.

State Abbreviations: Va. (traditional use); VA (post office use).

Capital City: Richmond became the capital city in 1780. Other capitals were Jamestown (1607-1699) and Williamsburg from 1699 to 1780.

Land Area: 39,598 square miles. Ranks 37th in size among all of the 50 states. (10th in size among the 14 Southern States.)

Population (1995 approximate): 6,400,000 people. Ranks 12th among all states.

Density: 162 people per square mile.
Distribution: 63% urban (city).   37% rural (non-city).

Largest City: Virginia Beach — approximate population is 400,000 people.

Highest Elevation: Mt. Rogers — 5,729 feet above sea level.

State Motto: "Sic semper tyrannis." (Thus always to tyrants.)

Important Historical Events: (a.) George Washington, a Virginian, became the first President of the United States in 1789. (b.) Virginia withdrew from the Union in 1861 and became the major battleground of the Civil War (1861-1865). (c.) General Robert E. Lee surrendered to General Grant at the Appomattox Courthouse on April 9, 1865, ending the Civil War.

Virginia's Animals ❖ Plants ❖ Symbols

Tree & Flower: American Dogwood   **Bird:** Cardinal

Shell: Oyster   **Dog:** American Foxhound

Song: "Carry Me Back to Old Virginia"

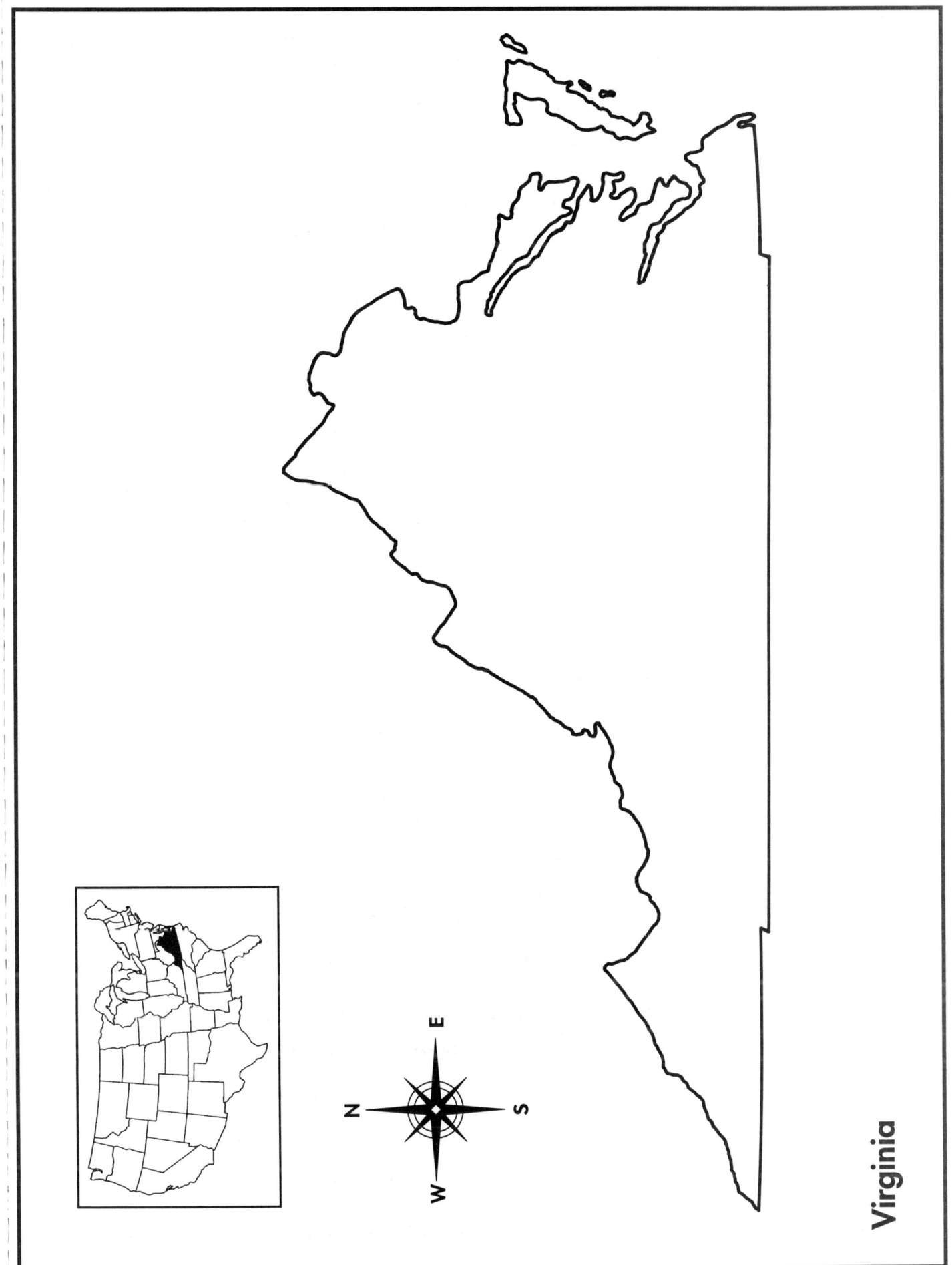

Washington
Evergreen State ❖ *Chinook State*

Name _____

Date _____

First Non-Native American Settlement:
Fort Okanogan was the first permanent settlement in the Washington region. It was founded by John Jacob Astor's fur company in 1811.

Organized as a Territory: March 2, 1853.

Admitted to the Union: November 11, 1889 — the 42nd state admitted into the Union.

Location: Northwestern Region of the United States — part of the Pacific Coast States.

State Abbreviations: Wash. (traditional use); WA (post office use).

Capital City: Olympia has been the capital of Washington since it became a state in 1889.

Land Area: 66,582 square miles.   Ranks 20th in size among all of the 50 states.
(3rd in size among the 3 Pacific Coast States.)

Population (1995 approximate): 5,300,000 people.   Ranks 15th among all states.

Density: 78 people per square mile.
Distribution: 73% urban (city).   27% rural (non-city).

Largest City: Seattle — approximate population is 540,000 people.

Highest Elevation: Mt. Rainier — 14,410 feet above sea level.

State Motto: "Alki." (By and By.)

Important Historical Event: On May 18, 1980, Mount Saint Helens volcano erupted. The eruption caused 60 deaths and enormous damage in the southwestern part of the state. Volcanic ash from the blast traveled hundreds of miles to the east.

Washington's Animals ❖ Plants ❖ Symbols

Bird: Willow Goldfinch   **Tree:** Wash. Hemlock

Colors: Green & Gold   **Flower:** Coast Rhododendron   **Fish:** Steelhead Trout

Gem: Petrified Wood   **Dance:** Square Dance

U.S. Outline Maps & State Studies: 100

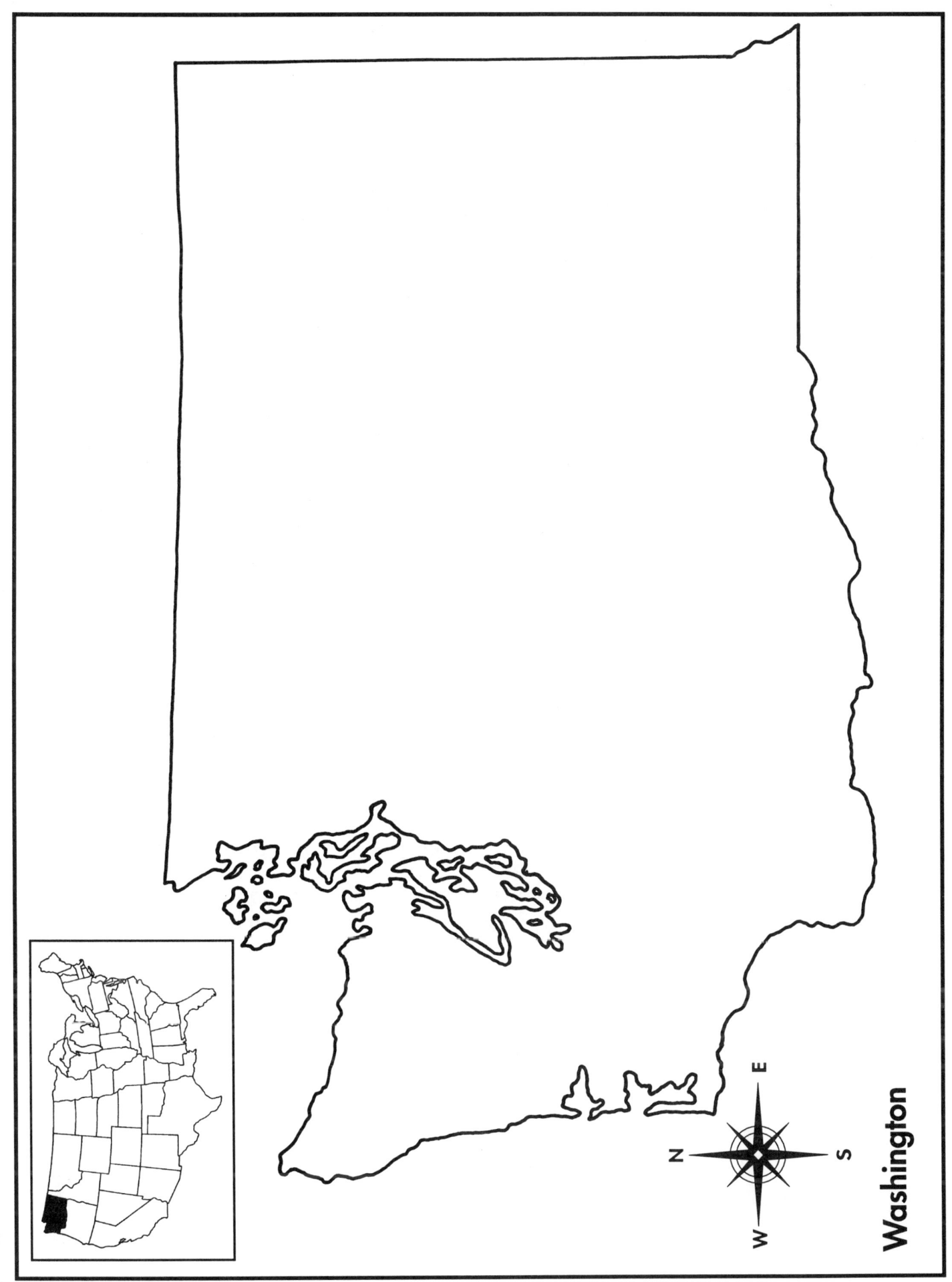

West Virginia

Mountain State

Name _____

Date _____

First Non-Native American Settlement:
    The first settler in the region was Morgan Morgan (Yes, Morgan Morgan) from Delaware. He built a log cabin in 1726, at the site of Bunker Hill. Germans came from Pennsylvania in 1727 to establish a settlement where Shepherdstown is today.

Organized as a Territory: West Virginia was never a territory of the United States.

Admitted to the Union: June 20, 1863 — the 35th state admitted into the Union.

Location: Eastern-Central Region of the United States — part of the Southern States.

State Abbreviations: W. Va. (traditional use); WV (post office use).

Capital City: Charleston became the capital city in 1885. It was also the capital from 1870 to 1875. Wheeling was the capital twice also (1863-1870 and 1875-1885).

Land Area: 24,087 square miles. Ranks 41st in size among all of the 50 states. (12th in size among the 14 Southern States.)

Population (1995 approximate): 1,875,000 people. Ranks 34th among all states.

    Density: 76 people per square mile.
    Distribution: 39% urban (city). 61% rural (non-city).

Largest City: Charleston — approximate population is 60,000 people.

Highest Elevation: Spruce Knob — 4,863 feet above sea level.

State Motto: *"Montani semper liberi."* (Mountaineers are always free.)

Important Historical Event: In 1861, the counties of western Virginia refused to separate from the Union with Virginia. These counties formed a separate government from Virginia's that supported the Union and non-slavery. (In 1915, the Supreme Court ruled that West Virginia had to pay Virginia $12.3 million for the cost of separating.)

West Virginia's Animals ❖ Plants ❖ Symbols

Bird: Cardinal   **Flower:** Rhododendron   **Tree:** Sugar Maple

Colors: Blue & Gold   **Animal:** Black Bear

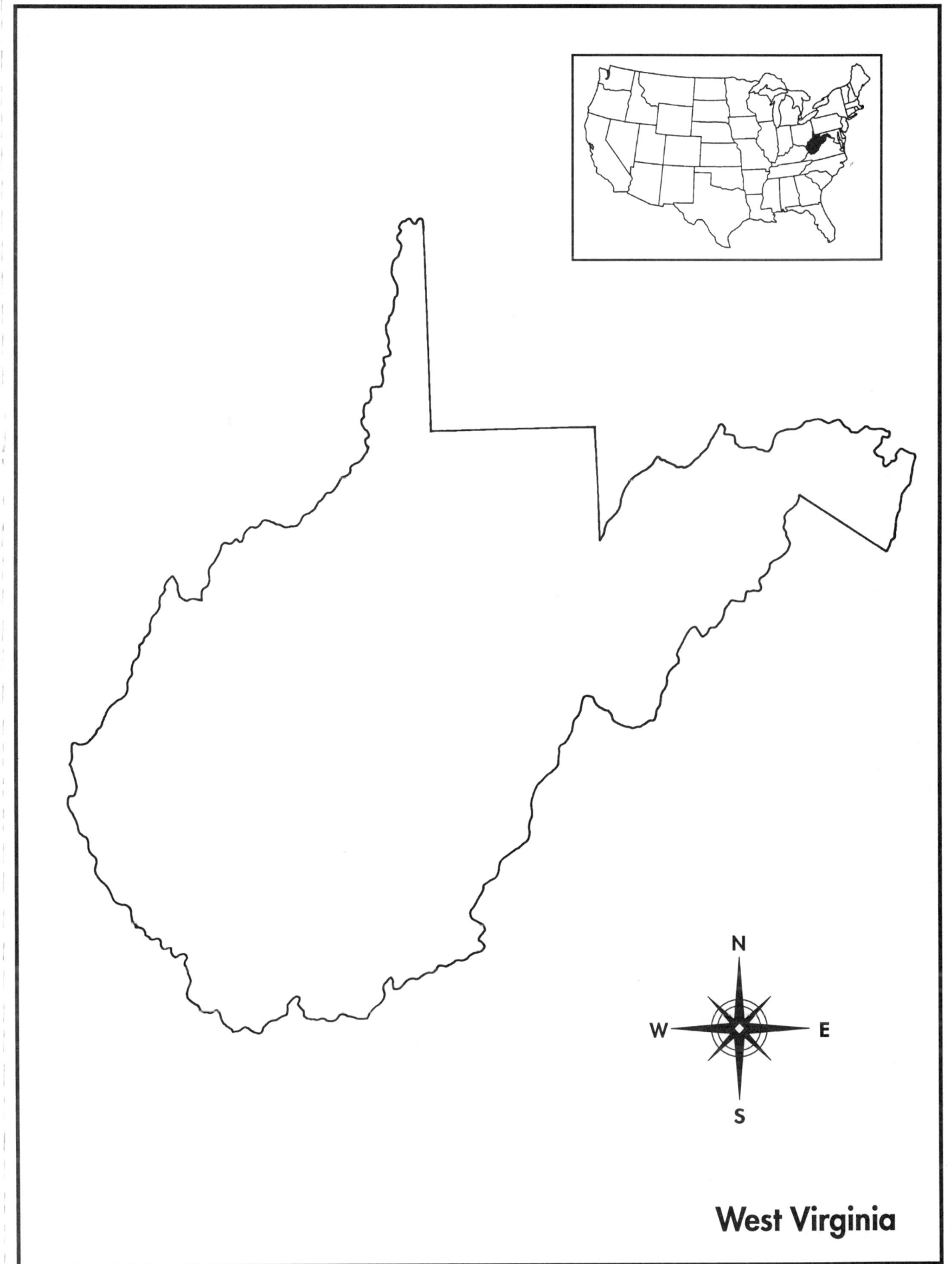

West Virginia

Badger State

Name _____

Date _____

First Non-Native American Settlement:
    The first missionary to the Wisconsin Indians arrived in the territory about 1660. Father René Ménard, a Roman Catholic priest, established a mission near present-day Ashland.

Organized as a Territory: July 4, 1836.

Admitted to the Union: May 29, 1848 — the 30th state admitted into the Union.

Location: North-Central Region of the United States — part of the Midwestern States.

State Abbreviations: Wis. (traditional use); WI (post office use).

Capital City: Madison has been the capital city since 1838. Territorial capitals were Belmont (1836) and Burlington, now a part of Iowa, from 1837 to 1838.

Land Area: 54,314 square miles. Ranks 25th in size among all of the 50 states. (10th in size among the 12 Midwestern States.)

Population (1995 approximate): 5,200,000 people. Ranks 17th among all states.

    Density: 93 people per square mile.
    Distribution: 66% urban (city).   34% rural (non-city).

Largest City: Milwaukee — approximate population is 650,000 people.

Highest Elevation: Timms Hill — 1,952 feet above sea level.

State Motto: "Forward."

Important Historical Events: (a.) The first hydroelectric plant in the U.S. was built at the rapids of the Fox River, near Appleton, in 1882. (b.) Cheese making was introduced commercially in Wis. by settlers from New York (1845). (c.) The first kindergarten in the U.S. was at Watertown in 1856. Only German-speaking kids attended.

Wisconsin's Animals ❖ Plants ❖ Symbols

Bird: Robin   **Beverage:** Milk   **Flower:** Wood Violet   **Grain:** Corn
Tree: Sugar Maple   **Animal:** Badger   **Fish:** Musky (Muskellunge)
Dog: American Water Spaniel   **Mineral:** Galena   **Insect:** Honeybee
Rock: Red Granite   **Soil:** Antigo Silt Loam   **Fossil:** Trilobite   **Peace:** Dove

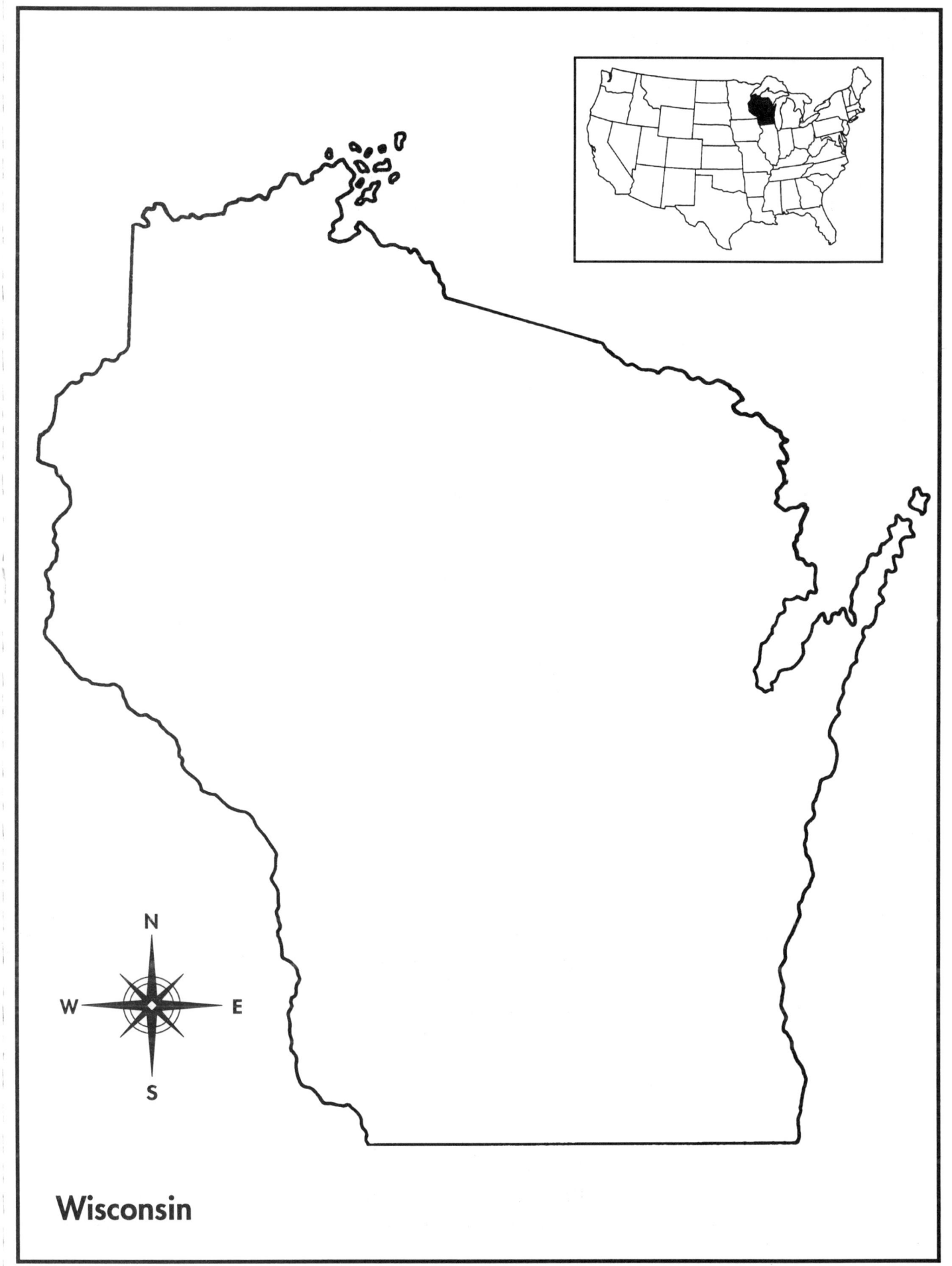

Equality State

Name _____

Date _____

First Non-Native American Settlement:
   In 1834, Fort Williams was established in what is now the eastern part of the state. However, in 1807, fur trader John Colter was the first white man to discover the geysers in the Yellowstone area. The Wyoming Territory soon became home to many trappers.

Organized as a Territory: May 19, 1869.

Admitted to the Union: July 10, 1890 — the 44th state admitted into the Union.

Location: Western-Central Region of the U.S. — part of the Rocky Mountain States.

State Abbreviations: Wyo. (traditional use); WY (post office use).

Capital City: Cheyenne became the capital city in 1869.

Land Area: 97,105 square miles.   Ranks 9th in size among all of the 50 states.
                                        (4th in size among the 6 Rocky Mountain States.)

Population (1995 approximate)**:** 475,000 people. Ranks 50th among all states.

   Density: 5 people per square mile.
   Distribution: 60% urban (city).   40% rural (non-city).

Largest City: Cheyenne — approximate population is 51,000 people.

Highest Elevation: Gannett Peak — 13,804 feet above sea level.

State Motto: "Equal Rights."

Important Historical Event: Trapper John Colter discovered *Yellowstone* in 1807. It was made the nation's first National Park in 1872. *Devils Tower*, in the Black Hills region, became a national monument in 1906. The rock is 1280 feet high.

Wyoming's Animals ❖ Plants ❖ Symbols

Flower: Indian Paintbrush   **Tree:** Cottonwood

Gemstone: Jade   **Bird:** Meadowlark

Insignia: Bucking Horse (Unofficial)